Language to go

ELEMENTARY

CONCORDE INTERNATIONAL
BUSINESS SCHOOL
ARNETT HOUSE
HAWKS LANE
CANTERBURY
KENT
ENGLAND
CT1 2NU

STUDENTS' BOOK

Simon le Maistre

Carina Lewis

Series Editor: Simon Greenall

Longman
v.longman.com

www.language-to-go.com

Vocabulary Personal information
Function Greetings
Grammar *To be: am, is, are*
Language to go Introducing yourself

Meeting people

Vocabulary

1 **Look at the form for an Internet café chat room. Put the words in the correct box.**

> doctor student single Poland
> businessman/woman learning English
> films the USA married Brazil
> music sport

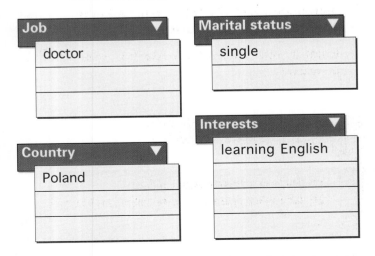

Job ▼
- doctor

Marital status ▼
- single

Interests ▼
- learning English

Country ▼
- Poland

Reading

2 **Read the e-mails and put them in the correct order. Write the numbers in the boxes.**

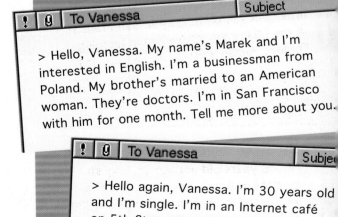

| ! | 🔋 | To Vanessa | | Subject |

> Hello, Vanessa. My name's Marek and I'm interested in English. I'm a businessman from Poland. My brother's married to an American woman. They're doctors. I'm in San Francisco with him for one month. Tell me more about you.

| ! | 🔋 | To Vanessa | | Subje |

> Hello again, Vanessa. I'm 30 years old and I'm single. I'm in an Internet café on 5th Street too! Where are you?

3 **Look at the photo on page 89. Where are Marek and Vanessa?**

4

Language focus

**4 Write the responses.
Use these expressions.**

> And you.   Bye.   Hi.
> Fine, thanks.

Example:
A: Nice to meet you.
B: _And you._

1 A: Hello.
  B: _____

2 A: How are you?
  B: _____

3 A: Goodbye.
  B: _____

5 a) 🔊 Listen and check your answers.

b) 🔊 Listen and repeat.

Practice

6 In pairs, practise the expressions.

Example:
A: *Nice to meet you.*
B: *And you.*

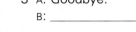

| ! | 🖇 | To Marek | | Subject |

> Hi. My name's Vanessa. I'm a doctor in Brazil but I'm on holiday in San Francisco in the USA. I am interested in learning English. Please write to me (in English!).

1

| ! | 🖇 | To Marek | | Subject |

> Hi Marek. Thank you for your e-mail. I'm 28 years old and I'm an English student in Brazil. I'm single and I'm interested in sport and films. Now I'm in an Internet café on 5th Street.

Grammar focus

7 Look at these sentences from e-mails.

I'm a businessman.
My name*'s* Vanessa.
He's married.
They're doctors.

I	'm (am)	single.
He/She/It	's (is)	from Brazil.
You/We/They	're (are)	doctors.

8 🔊 Listen and repeat.

Practice

9 Complete these sentences from e-mails.

Example: Hello! My name_'s_ Justine.

1 I _____ from France.
2 I _____ married and I have two children.
3 They _____ students.
4 Anna _____ interested in sport.
5 Michel _____ interested in learning English.
6 We _____ in the UK. Please e-mail me.

10 Write an e-mail about you. Write your name, country, job and interests.

Example: *My name's ...*

Get talking

11 Introduce yourself to other people in the class. Find someone to write e-mails to.

Example: *My name's Juan and I'm interested in music.*

Language to go

> I'm single and I'm interested in films.
> My brother's single and he's interested in films too!

> GRAMMAR REFERENCE PAGE 110
> PRACTICE PAGE 90

LESSON 2

Vocabulary   Everyday objects
Grammar   Plurals; *What is/are …?*
Language to go   Asking and answering: personal information

Personal details, please!

Vocabulary

1   **Write the number from the catalogue next to the correct word.**

watch ____	notebook ____
mobile phone ____	laptop ____
camera ____	bag ____
briefcase ____	diary ____
calculator ____	battery _1_
wallet ____	pen ____
dictionary ____	

2    **Listen to the words from Exercise 1 and mark the stress.**

Example: battery □

Grammar focus

3   **Look at the plural form of the nouns and complete the table.**

a camera – two camera**s**
a diary – two diar**ies**
a watch – two watch**es**

Singular	Plural
a wallet	wallets
a watch	
a dictionary	
a pen	
a battery	
a briefcase	

Listening

4   **Listen to a customer buy a present on the phone. Tick (✔) the correct information.**

Surname	Hanson	
Initials	P P	
Address	8 Kent Road, Bath	
Postcode	SN8 4LD	
Presents	a watch, a camera and a notebook	
Credit card number	0729 9456 3128	
Job	a businessman	
E-mail address	tp@hotmail.com.uk	

5   **Listen again and correct the mistakes.**

Perfect **Presents**

Perfec
Prese

Grammar focus

6 Look at the question form of the verb *be* and complete the table.

What's your surname? Hanson.
What are your initials? T P.

Singular	____'s	your credit card number?	0729 9456 3128
Plural	____ ____	they?	1 is a watch and 2 is a battery.

7 🔊 **Listen and repeat.**

job?
your job?
What's your job?

initials?
your initials?
What are your initials?

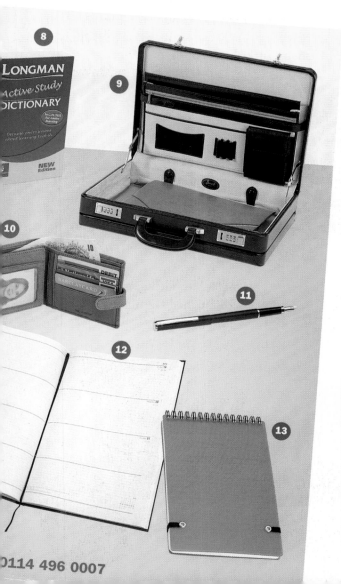

Practice

8 Write the questions.

Example: job
What's your job?

1 surname
2 initials
3 e-mail address
4 address
5 postcode
6 work and home phone numbers
7 presents

Get talking and writing

9 Choose two presents for yourself from the 'Perfect Presents' catalogue.

Student A: Phone Student B to buy the present.
Student B: Write the information on the form.
Now change roles.

Surname	
Initials	
Address	
Postcode	
Presents	
Credit card number	
Job	
E-mail address	

Language to go

A: What's your name?
B: My name's Bond.
   James Bond.

A: What's your number?
B: 007.

> GRAMMAR REFERENCE PAGE 110
> PRACTICE PAGE 90

Vocabulary   Nationalities and countries
Grammar   *To be* (questions and negatives)
Language to go   Asking about nationalities

Round the world

Vocabulary and speaking

1   Write the nationalities in the box next to the correct country in the table.

Chinese	Brazilian	
British	French	Polish
American	Turkish	
Japanese	Russian	

Country	Nationality
China	*Chinese*
Japan	_____
Germany	German
The USA	_____
Russia	_____
Argentina	Argentinian
Brazil	_____
Spain	Spanish
Poland	_____
Ireland	Irish
Turkey	_____
The UK	_____
Greece	Greek
France	_____
India	Indian

2   In pairs, test your partner.

Example:
A: France
B: French

Reading

3   Read the quiz and ⟨circle⟩ the correct answers.

Listening

4   🔊 Listen and check your answers to the quiz.

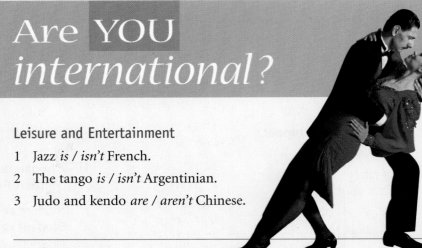

Are YOU international?

Leisure and Entertainment

1   Jazz *is* / *isn't* French.
2   The tango *is* / *isn't* Argentinian.
3   Judo and kendo *are* / *aren't* Chinese.

Food and Drink

1   Paella is   a) Italian b) Spanish c) French.
2   Sashimi and sushi are   a) Greek b) Japanese c) Russian.
3   Bigos is   a) Irish b) Turkish c) Polish.

Paella

Sushi

Famous People

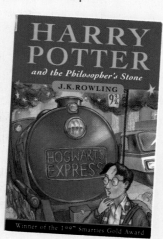

1   Is top model Gisele Bundchen German?
   a) Yes, she is.
   b) No, she isn't.

2   Is J K Rowling British?
   a) Yes, she is.
   b) No, she isn't.

3   Are Elton John and George Michael American?
   a) Yes, they are.
   b) No, they aren't.

Grammar focus

5 Look at these sentences and complete the tables of the verb *be*.

Jazz *is/isn't* French.
Judo and kendo *are/aren't* Chinese.

Is J K Rowling British?
a) *Yes, she is.* b) *No, she isn't.*

Are Elton John and George Michael American?
a) *Yes, they are.* b) *No, they aren't.*

Negatives		
I He/She/It We/You/They	'm not _____ _____	British. American. Chinese.

Questions			Short answers
Are	you	American?	Yes, I am. No, I'm not.
_____	she (he/it)	British?	Yes, she _____ . No, she _____ .
_____	they (we/you)	Chinese?	Yes, they _____ . No, they _____ .

Note: 'm not = am not
isn't = is not
aren't = are not

Practice

6 Rewrite the sentences to make them true.

Example:
J K Rowling is American. ✗ (British ✓)
J K Rowling isn't American. She's British.

1 Pizzas are Greek. ✗ (Italian ✓)
2 He's American. ✗ (Canadian ✓)
3 Baseball is Spanish. ✗ (American ✓)
4 You're Brazilian. ✗ (Argentinian ✓)
5 Seville oranges are French. ✗ (Spanish ✓)
6 She's English. ✗ (Irish ✓)

7 Complete the questions and answers.

Example:
She / the USA?
A: *Is she from the USA?*
Yes.
B: *Yes, she is.*

1 He / Italy?
A: _____
Yes.
B: _____

2 They / German?
A: _____
Yes.
B: _____

3 She / French?
A: _____
No.
B: _____

4 You / Polish?
A: _____
Yes.
B: _____

5 They / from Brazil?
A: _____
Yes.
B: _____

6 He / Argentina?
A: _____
No.
B: _____

Get writing and talking

8 In groups, write a class quiz. Use the quiz in Exercise 3 to help you.

1 Group A: Use the information on page 84.
 Group B: Use the information on page 87.

2 Find a partner from the other group and ask and answer your quiz questions.

Language to go

A: Are you British?
B: No, I'm not. I'm half Irish, half American.

> GRAMMAR REFERENCE PAGE 110
> PRACTICE PAGE 91

Vocabulary	Free time activities
Grammar	Possessive adjectives and possessive 's
Language to go	Talking about people and favourite things

Favourite things

Vocabulary

1 Tick (✓) the words in the box which you can see in the photos above.

> a market ✔   a shop   a film   a newspaper
> a restaurant   a TV programme   a magazine
> a book   a museum   a sport

2 Put the words from Exercise 1 in the correct column in the table.

to read	to go to	to watch
	a shop	

Listening

3 Listen and find out what these people like. Match each person to one of the photos above. Write the number of the photo next to the name.

Margarita ☐

David ☐   Min ☐   José ☐

Practice

6 **Complete the sentences with a possessive adjective or 's.**

Example: (they) _Their_ favourite restaurant is the Hard Rock Café.

1 (I) _____ name's Rachel.
2 This is (I) _____ friend.
3 (she) _____ name is Ana.
4 (we) _____ favourite shop is Zara.
5 John and Sue are (we) _____ friends.
6 John likes films. (He) _____ favourite film is *Terminator*.
7 (Sue) _____ favourite books are *Animal Farm* and *Dracula*.
8 Who are (you) _____ friends?
9 What is (they) _____ favourite activity?

Get talking

7 **Do the questionnaire about your favourite things.**

1 Add five more things from Exercise 1. Answer the questions about you.

Favourite ...	Me	Student 1	Student 2
shop			
food			
book			

2 Ask two students about their favourite things and complete the questionnaire.

Example: *What's your favourite film?*

3 Tell the class about your questionnaire.

Example: *Sarah's favourite film is 'Casablanca'.*

Grammar focus

4 **Look at the sentences and complete the table.**

1 It's *my* favourite shop.
2 *Her* favourite market is Borough Market.
3 *Its* food hall is excellent.
4 *Their* favourite is Burger King.
5 *Tim's* favourite is the Greek restaurant in *our* street.

Subject	Possessive
I	my
you	your
he	his
she	_____
it	_____
we	_____
they	_____
David	David's
Maria	_____

Note: *Tim's favourite* not ~~the favourite of Tim.~~

5 **Complete the rules with *his*, *her* or *their*.**

Use _____ for two or more people or things.
Use _____ for a woman.
Use _____ for a man.

Language to go

A: What's your favourite music?
B: Mozart.

> GRAMMAR REFERENCE PAGE 110
> PRACTICE PAGE 91

Vocabulary Activities: verbs and nouns
Grammar Present simple (positive)
Language to go Talking about family occasions

Celebrations

Vocabulary and speaking

1 Look at the photos on these pages of important celebrations. Where are they?

2 Match the verbs on the left with the groups of nouns on the right.

1 eat   a) salsa, to music, with someone
2 drink   b) a friend, your family
3 go   c) at eight o'clock, in the morning
4 visit   d) for a walk, to bed, to the temple
5 give   e) lunch, dinner, food
6 get up   f) ice cream, pizza, sushi
7 cook   g) cola, beer, water
8 play   h) a present, money
9 dance   i) a game, cards, an instrument

3 In pairs, describe the celebrations in the photos 1–3. Use the vocabulary from Exercise 2.

Example:
At Thanksgiving they eat a special lunch.
On New Year's Day …
At Carnival …

Reading

4 Read Amy's letter to her Japanese pen friend, Fumino, about Thanksgiving. Correct the statements below.

November 21

Dear Fumino,

Next week it's Thanksgiving. This is an important national holiday in the USA which we celebrate on the fourth Thursday in November. Everyone in my family eats all day – I love it! My mother gets up at six o'clock in the morning and she cooks the lunch. I get up at about ten o'clock and help my mother in the kitchen. All our family usually come for lunch. We have lunch at one o'clock and then play games. In the afternoon my father watches football on television. My mother goes for a walk. Here is a photo of our Thanksgiving lunch last year.

Example:
My mother gets up at ~~seven~~ o'clock. ✗ six

1 My father cooks lunch.
2 I get up at eight o'clock.
3 We have lunch at two o'clock.
4 My father goes for a walk.
5 My mother watches football on television.

③

Grammar focus

5 Look at the sentences from Amy's letter. Complete the two rules below for the present simple.

I *get up* at about ten o'clock.
She *cooks* lunch.
My father *watches* football.
We *have* lunch at one o'clock.

1 We add _____ to the verb with *he/she/it* in the present simple positive.

Example: eat → *eats*
cook → _____
play → _____

2 We add *-es* to *do*, *go* and verbs which end in *-ch, -ss, -sh, -x.*

Example: do → *does*
go → _____
watch → _____

Note: Look at the way the verb *have* changes:
We *have* breakfast at ten o'clock.
He *has* breakfast at ten o'clock.

Practice

6 a) 🔊 Look at the table for the pronunciation of the third person *-s*. Listen and repeat.

visit**s**	go**es**	watch**es**

b) 🔊 Listen to more verbs and write them in the correct columns in the table.

7 Read the sentences about Fumino's New Year's Day in Japan. <u>Underline</u> the correct forms of the verbs.

Example: We *get up* / *gets up* at six o'clock.

1 My father *go* / *goes* for a walk.
2 I *visit* / *visits* my friends in the morning.
3 My mother *cook* / *cooks* lunch.
4 My father *drink* / *drinks* sake.
5 We *eat* / *eats* a special fish dish, called osechi.
6 My brother usually *watch* / *watches* television.
7 Our parents *give* / *gives* us money.
8 I *play* / *plays* cards with my parents.

8 Read and talk about two celebrations.

Student A: Turn to page 84.
Student B: Turn to page 87.

Get talking ...

9 In pairs, describe a special (or typical) day.

Example: My special day is 25 December. I get up at nine o'clock.

... and writing

10 Write a letter to a pen friend and tell them about your special (or typical) day.

Language to go

A: We play cards, drink beer and watch TV.
B: And I cook, cook, cook!

> GRAMMAR REFERENCE PAGE 111
> PRACTICE PAGE 92

LESSON 6

Vocabulary   Activities: verbs and nouns
Grammar   Present simple (questions and negatives)
Language to go   Talking about ways of communicating

The modern world

Are you an Internet person?

1 Do you <u>use</u> the Internet?
  a) no ☐
  b) yes ☐

2 Do you _____ books
  a) on the phone? ☐
  b) on the Internet? ☐
  c) in a shop? ☐

3 Do you _____ a bank account
  a) on the phone? ☐
  b) on the Internet? ☐
  c) in a bank? ☐

4 Do you _____ a hotel
  a) on the phone? ☐
  b) on the Internet? ☐
  c) in a travel agent's? ☐

5 Do you _____ friends
  a) on the phone? ☐
  b) by e-mail? ☐
  c) in person? ☐

6 Do you _____ to music
  a) in cafés? ☐
  b) on the Internet? ☐
  c) on your phone? ☐

7 Do you _____ new people
  a) at work? ☐
  b) on the Internet? ☐
  c) in cafés? ☐

8 Do you _____ a course
  a) with a private teacher? ☐
  b) on the Internet? ☐
  c) in a class? ☐

Vocabulary and speaking

1 **Match the sentences below with the pictures A–C in the questionnaire.**

  1 They have meetings *in person*. ☐
  2 He studies *on the Internet*. ☐
  3 She's *on the phone*. ☐

2 **In pairs, say if you prefer to do things in person, by phone or on the Internet.**

3 **Complete the questionnaire about people and communication. Use the words in the box.**

buy	use	meet	contact	book
do	have	listen		

Listening

4 🎧 **Listen to Philip Scholes, an expert on communication and technology. Which two pictures in the questionnaire in Exercise 1 does he talk about?**

5 **Listen again and complete the statements with the percentages in the box.**

| 68% | 70% | 65% | 98% |

1 ____ of Europeans contact friends by e-mail.
2 ____ of Europeans contact friends by phone.
3 ____ of Europeans look for hotels on the Internet.
4 ____ of Europeans don't want to do a course on the Internet.

Grammar focus

6 **Look at these sentences and complete the rules in the table.**

Do Europeans *book* hotels on the Internet?
They *don't book* online.
How does your company *find* its information?
It *doesn't use* the Internet.

Negatives

I (You/We/They)	_____ (do not)	buy books online.
He (She/It)	_____ (does not)	meet people on the Internet.

Questions

_____ you use the Internet?	Yes, I do./No, I don't.
_____ she have a bank account?	Yes, she does./No, she doesn't.

7 🎧 **Listen and repeat.**

Do you
Do you use
Do you use the Internet?

Does he
Does he have a
Does he have a bank account?

Practice

8 **Complete the questions and answers.**

Example:
A: How *do you buy books*?
B: On the Internet. I *don't buy* (not buy) books in shops.

1 A: _____ at school?
  B: No, they _____ (not study) German. They study English.
2 A: When _____ ?
  B: In the evening. She _____ (not listen) to music in the morning.
3 A: _____ ?
  B: Yes, I do but I _____ (not use) the Internet to buy things.
4 A: Where _____?
  B: I _____ (not meet) new people in bars. I meet them at work.
5 A: _____ ?
  B: No, he _____ (not have) a bank account.
6 A: How _____?
  B: I _____ (not contact) friends by e-mail. I use the phone.

Get talking

9 **Find out if you are an Internet person.**

1 In pairs, do the questionnaire on page 14.

2 Now look at the key to the questionnaire. What kind of person are you/your partner?

Key

Mostly a)
● You are a phone person.
● It is important for you to do things quickly.

Mostly b)
● You are an Internet person.
● You like computers and technology and use the Internet to make life easy.

Mostly c)
● You prefer to do things in person.
● It's important for you to see people.

Language to go

A: Do you use the Internet?
B: No, I don't.

> GRAMMAR REFERENCE PAGE 111
> PRACTICE PAGE 92

Vocabulary   Objects you take on holiday; means of transport
Grammar   *A/an, some/any*
Language to go   Saying what you take on holiday and how you travel

Travelling

Vocabulary and speaking

1   **Write the numbers of the objects next to the words on the list.**

Things to take on holiday
walking boots   6
umbrella
map
sweaters
swimming trunks
towel
sunglasses
phrasebook
guide book
books to read
camera
film
alarm clock
personal stereo
CDs
credit card
travellers' cheques

2   **Look at the photo of Tim Hall, a photographer for travel guide books. In pairs, discuss the questions:**

1   Where do you think he goes on holiday?
2   What five things in Exercise 1 do you think he takes on holiday? What two things do you think he doesn't take on holiday?
3   Do you think he travels by plane, by bus or by train?

Reading and vocabulary

3   **Read about Tim Hall and check your answers to Exercise 2.**

4   **Complete the examples from the text.**

I always travel _____ plane from England …
On holiday I travel _____ train …
I never travel _____ bus …

TRAVELLING
with Tim Hall

I always take: a camera and a credit card. An alarm clock is important because I get up early to take good photos. I also take some sweaters – it can be cold at that time of the day! And I take some books to read.

I never take: a personal stereo because I like listening to the people when I'm in a different country. I don't take any guide books because they're very heavy!

I always travel: by plane from England to my destination. On holiday I travel by train, because I haven't got a lot of money.

I never travel: by bus because it's slow and it isn't comfortable.

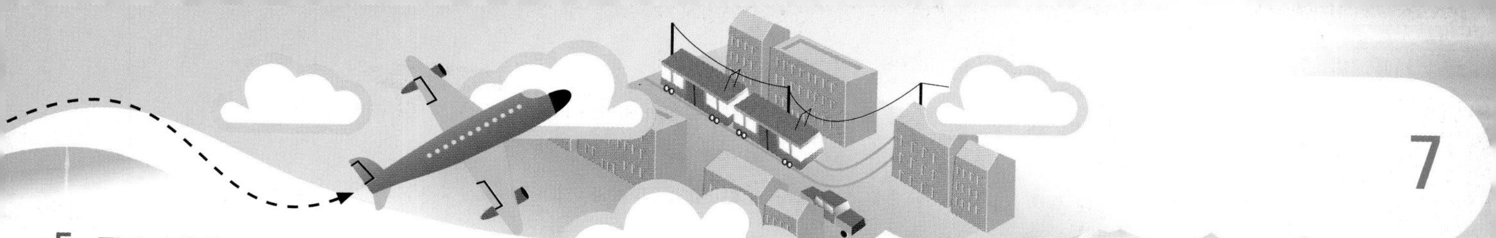

5 Tick (✓) the means of transport you can see above.

bus ☐   tram ☐   train ☐
bicycle ☐   car ☐   plane ☐   boat ☐
taxi ☐   underground (UK)/subway (US) ☐

6 Ask your partner these questions.

1 How do you travel on holiday?
2 How do you travel in your town?

Grammar focus

7 Look at the examples and complete the grammar rules for *a*, *an*, *some* and *any*.

I take *a* camera.
An alarm clock is important.
I take *some* books.
I don't take *a* personal stereo.
I don't take *any* guide books.
Do you take *any* books?

We use _____ or _____ when we talk about one thing (singular).
We use _____ when we talk about more than one thing (plural), but the number is not important.
We use _____ with plural negatives and questions.

Note: *an alarm clock*. We use *an* before a vowel sound.

8 a) 📼 Look at the sentences in Exercise 7. Listen to the pronunciation of *a*, *an*, *some*, and *any*.

b) Listen again and repeat.

Practice

9 Complete the sentences with *a*, *an*, *some* or *any*.

Example: I always take **a** towel.

1 Do you take _____ umbrella?
2 Peter usually takes _____ CDs.
3 I don't take _____ books.
4 Do you have _____ credit cards?
5 Martha wants to buy _____ sunglasses.
6 I always take _____ alarm clock.
7 Greg never takes _____ phrasebook.
8 My brother always takes _____ sweaters.

Get talking

St Lucia

Kenya

London

10 Make plans for travelling to the places in the photos.

1 For each of these places, choose:
- five things (from Exercise 1) that you want to take with you.
- how you want to travel from your home.
- how you want to travel when you are on holiday.

2 In pairs, decide what to take to each place, and how to travel.

Language to go

A: I usually travel by car and take some CDs!
B: What?

> GRAMMAR REFERENCE PAGE 111
> PRACTICE PAGE 93

LESSON 8

Vocabulary	Objects that people collect
Grammar	*Have got*
Language to go	Talking about possessions

The collectors

The biggest Garfield collection

Mike Drysdale and Gayle Brennan from California, USA, have got 3,000 Garfield souvenirs. Garfield is their favourite comic-strip character and their house is like a Garfield museum. They've got posters, toys, comics, clothes and ornaments in every room. They started their collection in 1994 when Gayle bought a Garfield bed for their cats.

Jim Davis created Garfield in 1978 and now 220 million people read the comic. However, Jim Davis hasn't got a cat because his wife doesn't like them.

Vocabulary and speaking

1 **In pairs, make a list of things which people collect.**

2 **Say which words you can see in the photo.**

> T-shirt   toy   poster   photo album
> postcard   plate   mug   picture
> ornament

Reading

3 **Read the text about Garfield. Complete the sentences with words from the box.**

> 220 million   Jim Davis
> Garfield   Mike and Gayle

1 _____ is a comic-strip character.
2 _____ collect Garfield souvenirs.
3 _____ writes Garfield.
4 _____ people read the comic.

Grammar focus

4 Look at these sentences and complete the table.

Mike and Gayle *have got* 3,000 Garfield souvenirs.
They *'ve got* posters, toys and comics.
Jim Davis *hasn't got* a cat.

Positive	I/You/We/They	've (have)	got	3,000 souvenirs.
	He/She/It	_____ (has)		a toy.
Negative	I/You/We/They	_____ (have not)	got	any toys.
	He/She/It	_____ (has not)		a cat.

Questions	_____	you		any toys?	Yes, I have. No, I haven't.
	_____	she	_____		Yes, she has. No, she hasn't.

Note: We use *have got* when we talk about possession.

Practice

5 📼 Listen and repeat.

1 I've got five photo albums.
2 He's got 50 postcards.
3 Have you got a photo collection?
4 Yes, I have.
5 No, I haven't.

6 Underline the correct form of *have got*.

Example: My friend *have got / has got* 2,000 Star Wars toys.

1 *Have got / Have you got* a T-shirt from Disneyland?
2 *I've / I's* got a good collection of books.
3 A: Have you got any interesting ornaments?
   B: Yes, *I've got / I have*.
4 We *haven't / hasn't* got a Garfield plate.
5 *Have you / You've* got any photo albums?
6 *She's got / She's* a special mug from Poland.
7 A: Have you got any postcards from Australia?
   B: No, I *haven't got / haven't*.
8 *He's / He've* got a poster of Michelle Pfeiffer.

Get talking

7 Talk about things you collect.

1 Answer the questionnaire 'Are you a collector?'.

2 In pairs, talk about your collections/special things.

Example:
A: Have you got a collection?
B: Yes, I have.
A: What have you got?
B: Books.
A: How many books have you got?
B: Five hundred.

ARE YOU A COLLECTOR?

What do you collect? Tick (✓) or cross (✗).		How many …?
books	☐	
CDs	☐	
photos	☐	
ornaments	☐	
mugs	☐	
plates	☐	
toys	☐	
posters	☐	
postcards	☐	
pictures	☐	
Others: _____		

What special things have you got in your house? _____

Why are they special?
_____

Language to go

A: How many postcards have you got?
B: I've got 600!

> GRAMMAR REFERENCE PAGE 111
> PRACTICE PAGE 93

19

Vocabulary   Sports
Grammar   Verbs + -*ing*
Language to go   Talking about sports you like/hate

Top sports

Vocabulary and speaking

1   **Write the sports in the box next to the correct verb.**

tennis   jogging   basketball   walking
volleyball   cycling   aerobics   football
skiing   golf   swimming   karate

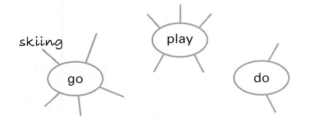

skiing

play

go

do

2   **Say which sports you can see in the photos.**

3   **Say which sports are popular in your country.**

Listening

4   **Look at the chart about popular sports in Canada. In pairs, discuss the percentage of people you think do each sport. Write the sports on the chart where you think they go.**

walking   jogging   basketball   cycling
swimming   aerobics

Popular sports in Canada						
Sports	0%	20%	40%	60%	80%	100%
basketball						
___						
___						
___						
___						

5   **Listen to a TV interview about the report. Check your answers to Exercise 4.**

6   **Listen again and complete the sentences with the words in the box.**

like   don't mind   love   don't like
hate   love

1 Canadians don't _____ doing sports.
2 Men _____ going jogging.
3 Women _____ playing team games.
4 They _____ doing aerobics.
5 Canadians _____ doing
   sport in general.
6 They _____
   walking.

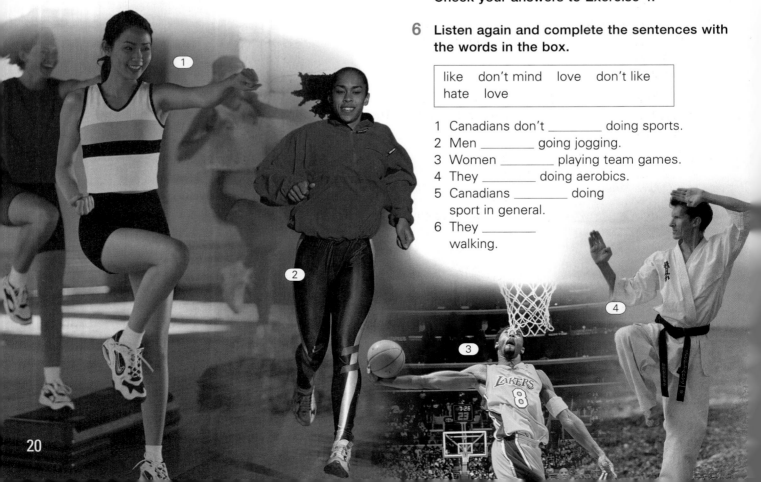

Grammar focus

7 a) Look at the verbs in the box in Exercise 6 and put them in the correct order.

_____   *don't like*   _____   _____   _____

b) Look at the examples and complete the rule.

I like *football.* (noun)
I like *playing golf.* (verb+-ing)

The verbs *hate, love, like* and *don't mind* are followed by a _____ or a _____ + *-ing.*

Practice

8 Complete the dialogues. Use the correct forms of the words in brackets.

Example:
A: What sports do you *like doing* (like/do)?
B: I don't really like sports but *I don't mind swimming* (not mind/swim).

1 A: Do your parents do any exercise?
   B: Yes, my father _____ (love/play golf) and my mother _____ (like/walk).

2 A: Do you like jogging?
   B: No, I _____ (hate/jog). I think it's boring. What about you?
   A: I love it!

3 A: Do they _____ (hate/do) any sports?
   B: Yes, they _____ (not like/play football). They're not very good at it!

4 A: Do you _____ (like/do aerobics)?
   B: Yes, I do. I go to a class at work.

5 A: Does he _____ (like/ski)?
   B: Yes, he _____ (love/it). He goes every weekend.

Get talking

9 Find the most popular sports in your class.

1 Write five more sports on the notepad below.

2 Ask other students in the class about their favourite sports. Mark one point for each person who *likes* the sport.
   Example:
   A: *Do you like swimming?*
   B: *Yes, I love it.*
   (1 point)

Favourite sports

swimming   /

_____

_____

_____

_____

_____

3 Tell the class which of the sports in your list scored the most points. What is the most popular sport in your class?

5
6

Language to go

A: Do you like jogging?
B: No, I hate it, but I love watching TV!

> GRAMMAR REFERENCE PAGE 112
> PRACTICE PAGE 94

Vocabulary	Clothes
Function	Asking for information in a shop
Language to go	Shopping for clothes

Shopping

Vocabulary and speaking

1 **In pairs, discuss these questions.**

Do you like shopping for clothes?
Where do you buy your clothes?
Do you like shopping with friends or alone?

2 **Find these clothes in the picture.**

shirt ____	T-shirt ____	trousers ____
skirt ____	shorts ____	sweater _2_
jacket ____	suit ____	trainers ____
shoes ____	boots ____	coat ____

3 **Complete the headings in the table with the words in the box.**

medium   small   large

Size conversion table			
	_____	_____	_____
Women British American European	10 8–10 40	12 10–12 42	14 12–14 44
Men British/American European	38 48	40 50	42 52

Listening

4  **Listen to a conversation in a department store. <u>Underline</u> the correct answer.**

The customer wants:
1 a sweater in *small / medium / large*.
2 *shorts / trousers / a skirt* in size 12.
3 a *blue / green / red* skirt.
The coat costs:
4 *£100 / £500 / £1,000*.

Language focus

5 **Say what information the questions ask for. Write the words in the correct place.**

price   colour   size   other

Have you got this sweater in large? Have you got these trousers in size 12? What size are you?	
How much is it/are they? How much is this/are these?	
Have you got this watch in blue? What colour do you like?	
Can I help you? Can I try it on?	other

Note: Look at the shop assistant's responses:
Here you are.
Yes, of course.
No, sorry.

Practice

6 **Look at the table in Exercise 5 and complete the shopping expressions.**

Example: Shirt in small?
        Have you got this shirt in small?

1 Help?
2 Suit in large?
3 Here.
4 Try it on?
5 Colour?
6 Bag in brown?
7 No.
8 How much / pens?
9 Coat in medium?
10 How much / diary?

7  **Listen and repeat.**

How much is it?
Can I try it on?
Can I help you?
Have you got it in blue?

8 **In pairs, practise the shop dialogue below. Choose one item of clothing to buy.**

Example:
A: Can I help you?
B: How much is this suit?

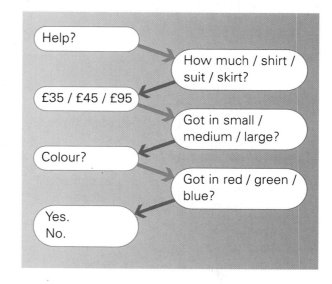

Help?

How much / shirt / suit / skirt?

£35 / £45 / £95

Got in small / medium / large?

Colour?

Got in red / green / blue?

Yes.
No.

Get talking

9 **In pairs, read the information and roleplay the conversation in the shop.**

1 Student A: It is your birthday and you want to buy some presents for yourself. Look at the photos on page 84 and decide what you want to buy.

  Student B: You are a shop assistant in the department store. Look at page 87 for the items you have and the prices.

2 Tell the rest of the class what you bought.

Language to go

A: Can I help you?
B: Have you got this in large, medium *and* small?

> GRAMMAR REFERENCE PAGE 112
> PRACTICE PAGE 94

Vocabulary Adjectives to describe places in a town
Grammar *There is/are*
Language to go Talking about places you know

Interesting places

Vocabulary and speaking

1 **Complete the sentences about Portobello Market.**

friendly   delicious   cheap   busy   interesting

Example: Tourists go to Portobello Market because it's *interesting*.

1 The clothes are _____ . For example, you can buy a shirt for £1.
2 The people are _____ . They always talk to you.
3 I love the street food. It's _____ .
4 It's _____ on Saturday. There are lots of people.

2 **Match the adjectives on the left with the opposites on the right.**

1 cheap   a) unfriendly
2 busy   b) bad
3 big   c) quiet
4 friendly   d) expensive
5 interesting   e) small
6 good   f) boring

3 **In pairs, describe the photos of Portobello Market. Use the adjectives in Exercise 2.**

Reading

4 **Read about Portobello Market. Are the statements true (T) or false (F)?**

1 There's a big museum. ☐

2 There's a market on Thursday. ☐

3 There aren't any cafés. ☐

4 The music in the Market Bar is good. ☐

Address: http://www.realplaces.com.uk   ▸ go

Yahoo! UK & Ireland   Products for Mac   Microsoft Internet Explorer   Microsoft Outlook Express   Microsoft Office   Microsoft   Apple

Favorites   History   Search   Scrapbook   Page Holder

'Real places by real people'

Don't listen to the travel agents.
Listen to the people who live there.

Portobello Market
by Simon Bean,
London W11.

I love Portobello. It's one of London's main tourist attractions. There aren't any big museums but there's an interesting market on Friday and Saturday. You can buy everything from fruit and vegetables to cheap clothes, CDs and books.

Are there any good places for food? Yes! There are lots of cheap cafés on Golborne Road. My favourite is the Portuguese café. You get good coffee and delicious cakes there.

There are some good restaurants and the bars are always busy at the weekend. I love the Market Bar because the music is good and there's a friendly atmosphere.

Grammar focus

5 Look at the sentences and complete the rules.

There's an interesting market.
There are some good restaurants.
There aren't any big museums.
Are there any good places for food?
Yes, *there are.*/No, *there aren't.*

Positive
We use *there* + _____ + singular nouns.
We use *there* + _____ + plural nouns.

Negative
We use *there* + <u>isn't</u> + singular nouns.
We use *there* + _____ + plural nouns.

Questions
We use <u>Is</u> + *there* ...? with singular nouns.
We use _____ + *there* ...? with plural nouns.

Practice

6 Look at the picture and complete the description.

Example: people
     There are some people.

1 a small bar	4 cheap hotel
2 market	5 good cafés
3 museums	6 interesting shops

7 a) 🔊 **Listen and check your answers.**

b) Listen again and repeat.

8 In pairs, look at two different pictures. Ask questions to find six differences in the pictures.

Student A: Look at the picture on page 84.
Student B: Look at the picture on page 87.

Example:
A: **Is there a big hotel?**
B: **No, there isn't.**

Get talking ...

9 Ask your partner about a special place they know. Make notes.

Ask about:
• the shops
• places to eat and drink
• things to do.

Example:
A: **Are there any cheap cafés?**
B: **Yes, there are.**

... and writing

10 Write a review of your partner's special place for the 'Real places' website. Use the information from Exercise 9.

Language to go

A: Are there any good cafés here?
B: Yes, there are.

> GRAMMAR REFERENCE PAGE 112
> PRACTICE PAGE 95

LESSON 12

Vocabulary Everyday activities
Grammar Adverbs of frequency
Language to go Talking about how often you do things

The weekend

Vocabulary and speaking

1 **Complete the texts 1–3 with the words in the boxes.**

go to the beach   go to church   meet friends

1 On Sundays I <u>go to church</u> in the mornings. After that I _____ and it's good to talk about the week. I sometimes _____ and swim in the sea.

go to the gym   stay in   watch a film

2 On Saturday mornings I like doing exercise so I _____ . In the evenings we _____ with the family and we _____ on television.

go for a drink   get a takeaway   work late

3 I _____ on Friday nights because I want to finish my work before the weekend. I then _____ in the bar near the office. I don't have time to cook so I _____ on the way home.

2 **In pairs, match the texts 1–3 to the photos. Talk about which activities in Exercise 1 you like doing.**

Listening

3  **Listen to the radio programme about free time activities round the world. Find the photo that each speaker describes.**

Speaker 1 _____
Speaker 2 _____

4 **Listen again and <u>underline</u> the correct statements.**

1 Hiroko often *stays in / works late* on Fridays.
2 She usually goes *for a drink / to a restaurant*.
3 She never *cooks / gets a takeaway*.
4 Marcelo always goes *to the gym / to the beach* on Sundays.
5 He sometimes *eats / cooks* lunch in the Old Town.

Grammar focus

5 **a) Write the adverbs of frequency in the correct place on the scale.**

often   always   sometimes   never   usually

100% _____

_____

_____

sometimes

0% _____

b) Look at the sentences. Then <u>underline</u> the correct words to complete the rules.

I *often work* late on Friday.
We *always go* to the beach.
It *is always* busy.

The adverb comes *before / after* the verb.
The adverb comes *before / after* the verb be.

c) Choose the correct adverb of frequency to complete the question.

How _____ do you stay in?

Practice

6 **Complete the sentences with a verb and the adverb of frequency in brackets.**

Example:
A: What do you do on Saturday mornings?
B: I *usually go* to the gym. (usually)

1 A: My boss _____ late on Fridays. Do you? (often)
  B: No, never. I _____ for a drink with friends. (always)
2 A: Do you usually go out on Saturday night?
  B: No. The bars _____ busy. (usually)
3 A: How _____ do you _____ a takeaway?
  B: I _____ a takeaway on Sundays. (sometimes)
4 A: I _____ in on Saturday nights. Do you? (never)
  B: Yes, I _____ a film at home. (sometimes)

7 **Complete the sentences about your weekend.**

Example: I never <u>go to the gym</u> on <u>Sundays</u>.

1 I usually _____ on _____ .
2 I always _____ on _____ .
3 I never _____ on _____ .
4 I often _____ on _____ .
5 I sometimes _____ on _____ .

Get talking

8 **Find out what people in your class do at the weekend.**

1 Ask other people in your group what they usually do. Use the vocabulary in Exercise 1 to help you.

   Example:
   A: Do you meet friends at the weekend?
   B: Yes.
   A: How often?
   B: Always.

2 Complete the table below with the information you learn.

   Example: <u>25%</u> always <u>go to a restaurant on Saturdays.</u>

Class survey

%	frequency	activity
....	usually	....
....	always	....
....	never	....
....	often	....
....	sometimes	....

3 Tell the class about your survey.

Language to go

A: How often do you work late?
B: Never!

> GRAMMAR REFERENCE PAGE 112
> PRACTICE PAGE 95

Vocabulary	Furniture in an office/living room
Grammar	Prepositions of place
Language to go	Telling someone where things are in a room

Office ... or living room?

Vocabulary

1 Write the numbers in the picture next to the correct words in the box.

sofa ___	desk _4_
lamp ___	bookcase ___
bin ___	chair ___
plant ___	printer ___
cupboard ___	telephone ___
calendar ___	armchair ___
computer ___	stereo ___

2 a) Count the syllables in the words from Exercise 1. Then complete the table.

□	□ □	□ □ □	□ □ □
bin plant lamp chair desk			

b) Practise saying the words with your partner.

28

Listening

3  Listen to Christine telling the men where to put the furniture. <u>Underline</u> the correct answer in this statement.

She *is / isn't* sure about where she wants the furniture in her new office.

4 Listen again and tick (✓) the items of furniture in Exercise 1 which they talk about.

Grammar focus

5 Look at the sentences and say where the ball is. Write the prepositions next to the correct pictures.

Put the desk *in front of* the window.
I'd like the computer *on* the desk, please.
There's a stereo *in* the cupboard.
Put the armchair *opposite* the desk.

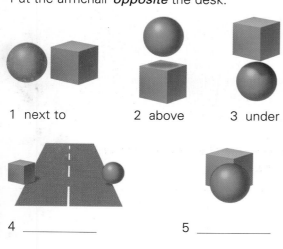

1 next to   2 above   3 under

4 _____   5 _____

6 _____   7 _____

Practice

6 Look at the picture of the room in Exercise 1 and correct the prepositions.

Example:
There's a sofa ~~opposite~~ the door ✗ next to

1 The telephone's *in front of* the desk.
2 There's a bin *next to* the desk
3 I've got the stereo *on* the cupboard.
4 There's a plant *in front of* the sofa.
5 The printer's *next to* the desk.
6 There's a cupboard *above* the bookcase.
7 I've got my favourite armchair *next to* the desk.
8 There's a calendar *opposite* the sofa.

7 Look at the picture of the room in Exercise 1. In pairs, ask and answer questions about the following items.

Student A	Student B
bookcase	books
lamp	bin
plant	armchair
calendar	computer

Example:

A: Where's the desk?
B: It's in front of the window.
A: Is there a plant on the table?
B: Yes, there is.
A: Has she got the cupboard next to the door?
B: No, she hasn't. It's under the bookcase.

Get talking

8 Draw a plan of your office or living room and give it to your partner. Do not draw the furniture.

1 Student A: Describe your room.
   Student B: Draw the furniture in the correct place.

2 Change roles.

Language to go

A: Where's the phone?
B: It's on the desk –
   I think.

> GRAMMAR REFERENCE PAGE 112
> PRACTICE PAGE 96

Vocabulary Family
Grammar Present continuous for now
Language to go Talking about what your family/friends are doing

Family

Vocabulary and speaking

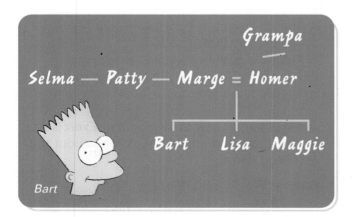

Grampa

Selma — Patty — Marge = Homer

Bart Lisa Maggie

Bart

1 **Look at the Simpson family tree and complete the sentences.**

| brother father aunts grandfather |
| daughters children husband son |
| wife sisters parents mother uncle |

Example: Marge is my *wife.*

Homer

1 We have three _____ .
2 My _____ are Maggie and Lisa.
3 My _____ is Bart.
4 Grampa is my _____ .

5 Homer is my _____ .
6 My _____ are Selma and Patty.

Marge

Maggie

7 Bart is my _____ .
8 My _____ are Homer and Marge.
9 Marge is my _____ .

10 I've got two _____ , Selma and Patty.
11 My mother hasn't got any brothers so I haven't got an _____ .
12 Grampa is my _____ .

Lisa

2 **Draw your family tree and describe it to your partner.**

Reading

3 **a) Look at the picture of the Simpsons. Who do you think is happy watching television?**

   b) Read the letter to check your answers.

4 **Read the letter again and mark the statements true (T) or false (F).**

1 Bart doesn't like the television programme. ☐
2 Homer wants to be in Moe's bar. ☐
3 Marge is happy because her sisters are staying. ☐
4 Lisa wants to talk to the family. ☐

Readers' Letters

You

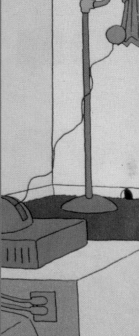

My favourite Simpsons programme is 'A Night at Home with the Family'. I love the moment when the family are sitting on the sofa together and they are watching television. Bart's very happy because he's sitting on everyone and is watching his favourite programme. But his parents and his sisters aren't so happy…

… Homer isn't happy because he isn't talking to his friends at Moe's Bar. Marge isn't happy because her sisters are staying and they're smoking in her kitchen. Maggie isn't watching television because she's looking at Bart. And Lisa … is she enjoying herself? No, she isn't. She's very unhappy because the family aren't talking – they are just watching television!

C BROWN, LIVERPOOL

Grammar focus

5 Look at the sentences and complete the rules.

He*'s watching* his favourite television programme.
They*'re smoking* in the kitchen.
Maggie *isn't watching* television.
Is she *enjoying* herself?
No, she *isn't.* / Yes, she *is*.

We use the present continuous to describe what is happening now.
We make the present continuous with:
_____ + verb + *-ing*.

6 Look at the spelling rules for the *-ing* form and complete the examples.

1 watch → watch*ing*
   talk → _____
2 have → ha*ving*
   smoke → _____
3 sit → si*tting*
   get → _____

V favourites ...

Practice

7  **Listen and find out what the Cormack family are doing. Complete the sentences.**

Example: Mr Cormack *'s getting up* .

1 His wife _____ .
2 His son _____ .
3 His daughter _____ .
4 Mr Cormack _____ .
5 The children _____ .

8 Complete the sentences. Use the correct form of the verbs in brackets.

Example: It's eight o'clock. **Are you getting up**?
         (you/get up)

1 A: What are you doing?
  B: I _____ breakfast. (cook)
2 A: _____ coffee? (drink)
  B: No, I'm not. It's tea.
3 A: Where _____? (you/go)
  B: To work.
4 A: Who _____ to? (she/talk)
  B: Her mother.
5 A: What are they doing now?
  B: They _____ football. (play)
6 A: Are you watching 'The Simpsons'?
  B: No, I _____ a film. (watch)

Get talking

9 In pairs, look at two different pictures. Ask questions to find five differences.

Student A: Look at the Cormacks on page 85.
Student B: Look at the Cormacks on page 88.

Example:
A: **Is the son watching TV?**
B: **No, he isn't. He's ...**

Language to go

A: What's your brother doing now?
B: He's doing his homework.

> GRAMMAR REFERENCE PAGE 112
> PRACTICE PAGE 96

LESSON 15

Vocabulary   Food and drink
Function   Making requests
Language to go   Ordering food and drink in a café

In a café

Vocabulary and speaking

1   Write the numbers from the picture of the café next to the food and drink on the menu below.

2    Listen to the dialogues in a café and complete the prices on the menu.

3   You have $8. Choose what you want to eat and drink from the menu. How much does it cost?

Listening

4   Listen to two friends order lunch from the menu. Circle what they order.

Example: a) coffee   b) tea

1 a) an apple   b) a banana
2 a) a cheese and tomato sandwich
   b) a chicken and tomato sandwich
3 a) tea with lemon   b) cola
4 a) a cheese sandwich
   b) a ham sandwich

Language focus

5   Look at the sentences and complete the table with *will* or *can*.

I'll have a coffee, please.
We'll have a small tea with lemon.
Can I have a large coffee?

I We	'll (_____)	have a coffee.
_____	I	have a tea?

6   a) Listen and circle the polite requests.

Example:
Can I have a chicken sandwich?   a)   b)

1 I'll have a cola.   a)   b)
2 We'll have a coffee.   a)   b)

b)   Listen and repeat the polite requests.

Liberty Café

Sandwiches:

1 chicken (with lettuce) $5.50
   ham (with lettuce) $5.95
   cheese (with lettuce) $____
   Extra: tomato $0.50

Cake: chocolate $____

Hot drinks:

tea *with lemon*   Small $____   Large $1.80
coffee *with cream*   Small $1.60   Large $____
hot chocolate   Small $1.70   Large $2.00

Cold drinks: cola/juice $____

Fruit: apple/banana $____

Practice

7 Look at the dialogues and <u>underline</u> the correct form.

Example: *Can I / I can* help you?

1 A: Are you ready to order?
B: Yes, *I / I'll* have a chicken, lettuce and tomato sandwich.
A: Anything else?
B: Yes, can I *have / to have* a cola, please?

2 A: Can *I / you* take your order?
B: Yes, can *I have / have I* a tea?
A: Small or large?
B: Large, please.
A: Is that all?
B: No, *I'll have / I want* a piece of banana cake, please.

3 A: Good morning.
B: Good morning. *Can I / I can* have a coffee with cream?
A: Yes, here you are.
B: And *I / I'll* have an apple, please. How much is that?

8 In pairs, practise the dialogues from Exercise 7.

Get talking

9 Roleplay a situation in a café.

Student A: You are a waiter/waitress in a café. Turn to page 85.
Student B: You are a customer. Turn to page 88.
Go to the different cafés to find the food and drink on your card. How much does it cost?

Language to go

A: Can I take your order?
B: I'll have a large coffee, please.

> GRAMMAR REFERENCE PAGE 113
> PRACTICE PAGE 97

Vocabulary Activities at work
Grammar *Can* for ability
Language to go Asking about job skills

Job skills

Vocabulary

1 **Complete the sentences. Use the verbs in the box.**

repair	read	drive	manage	sing
speak	type	design		

Example: I want to _design_ a website for people to book online.

1 It's important to _____ maps correctly.
2 My job is to _____ tanks when they don't work.
3 In the evening the guests _____ karaoke.
4 I need to _____ German to some of our guests.
5 I _____ cars and tanks.
6 Our receptionist can _____ 60 words a minute.
7 I _____ a team of 20 soldiers.

2 **Look at the people in the photos. Who would say each sentence in Exercise 1?**

1 _Amy_   5 _____
2 _____   6 _____
3 _____   7 _____
4 _____

Reading

3 **Read the 'Changing Jobs' web page and complete the sentences about Amy and Gary.**

1 _____ likes the new job.
2 _____ doesn't like the new job.

4 **Read the text again and complete the sentences with *Amy* or *Gary*.**

1 _____ can speak French.
2 _____ can't understand the guests.
3 _____ can drive a car.
4 _____ can't read maps.
5 _____ can't sing.

Grammar focus

5 **Look at the sentences in Exercise 4 and complete the tables for the forms of *can*.**

Positive	I/You/He/She/ We/They	_____	drive a car.
Negative		_____	

Questions and short answers	_____ you type?	Yes, I can.
		No, I can't.

File   Edit   View   Favorites   Tools   Help

Back   Forward   Stop   Refresh   Home   Search   Fav

Address http://www.changingjobs.com.uk

Changing Job

Are you in the perfect job or do you want to change? Each week, we help people decide on a new career. Try a new job for one week and decide if you want to make a permanent change.

Amy Renfrew is a professional soldier and tank driver. This week she is changing jobs with Gary Hampton, a hotel manager from Leeds. Can she become the perfect hotel manager?

'This is basically the worst week of my life. Gary can speak French and German and is really good with the guests but I can only say "Guten Morgen". The problem is we have a group of German guests tonight and I can't understand anything they say. Tonight is also cabaret night with karaoke. Usually the manager does the first song but I can't sing. Never again!'

Done

Start   Outbox - Outlook Expr...   Document1 - M

6 a) 🎧 **Listen to the pronunciation of *can*.**

I can speak French.
I can't sing.
Can you speak German?
Yes, I can.
No, I can't.

b) Listen again and repeat.

7 🎧 **Listen and <u>underline</u> the form you hear.**

Example: I *can / can't* read a map.

1 He *can / can't* design a website.
2 She *can / can't* repair a car.
3 *Can / Can't* you type?
4 We *can / can't* speak French.

Practice

8 Write complete questions and answers with *can/can't*.

Example:
A: You / read map?   B: Yes.
A: *Can you read a map?*   B: *Yes, I can.*

1 A: You / drive tank?   B: No.
2 A: You / type?   B: Yes.
3 A: He / speak French?   B: Yes.

Get talking

9 Interview your partner and complete the 'Changing Jobs' form.

Changing Jobs

	Yes	No
Administration		
Type		
Speak a foreign language		
Repair a photocopier		
I T (Information Technology)		
Write a computer programme		
Design a website		
Repair a computer		
Business		
Manage a company		
Write a business plan		
Manage your time		
Arts/Entertainment		
Dance		
Sing		
Play an instrument		

Which career is good for your partner?
Does your partner agree with your advice?

E CAREER CONSULTANTS

Gary Hampton is a hotel manager from Leeds and is married with two children. Can Gary become the perfect soldier?

't's cold, it's six o'clock in the morning, we're in the middle of a forest, but I actually quite like this job. can drive a car but it's difficult learning to drive a ank. I can also repair cars which is useful, because we ometimes have problems with the tank. The only roblem is that I can't read maps, so I think at the oment we're lost!'

Language to go

A: Can you read a map?
B: No, I can't.

> GRAMMAR REFERENCE PAGE 113
> PRACTICE PAGE 97

35

Vocabulary	Question words
Grammar	Past simple of *be:* was, were
Language to go	Talking about childhood memories

Memories

Vocabulary and speaking

1 **Complete the questions with the correct question word.**

How much   Where   When   How
How many   Who   What

Example: _How many_ telephone numbers can you remember?

1 _____ is your best friend's birthday?
2 _____ is your best friend's telephone number?
3 _____ old is your best friend?
4 _____ is your passport or identity card now?
5 _____ does a litre of milk cost?
6 _____ are the actors in your favourite television programme?

2 **In pairs, ask and answer the questions in Exercise 1 to see if you have a good memory.**

Listening

3  **Listen to two friends play 'The Memory Game'. Tick (✓) the questions they ask.**

1 Best holiday? ☐
2 Best friend at school? ☐
3 First girlfriend? ☐
4 First English lesson? ☐

4 **Listen again. Underline the answers they give to the questions.**

1 Greece / Germany
2 14 / 16
3 Ana / Emma
4 14 / 16

Grammar focus

5 **a) Look at the sentences and complete the table for the past simple of the verb *be*.**

I *was* sixteen years old.
We *were* young.
There *wasn't* a lot to do.
There *were* beautiful beaches.

I/He/She/It	_____ (+) wasn't (−)	fourteen years old.
There	_____ (+) _____ (−)	a lot to do.
We/You/They	_____ (+) weren't (−)	young.
There	_____ (+) _____ (−)	beautiful beaches.

b) Complete the question forms with the past simple form of *be*.

How old _____ you?
Where _____ your best holiday?

6  **Listen and repeat.**

A: Was it a good holiday?
B: Yes, it was.
A: How old were you?
B: I was ten.
A: Were the beaches good?
B: Yes, they were.

START → FINISH

Where ... your best holiday?

Who .... with?

Who ... your best friend at school?

What ... he / she interested in?

17

WHEN YOU WERE A CHILD

What ... your favourite food?

What ... your favourite drink?

Where ... your first school?

.. it a big school?

THE MEMORY GAME

WHEN YOU WERE TEN YEARS OLD

What ... you interested in?

What ... your most important possession?

When ... your first English lesson?

How many people ... in your class?

Who ... your first girlfriend / boyfriend?

How old ... you?

What ... your best present?

Who ... it from?

What ... your favourite subject at school?

Who ... the teacher?

Practice

7 **Complete the dialogues with the past of be.**

Example:
A: _Was_ it a good holiday?
B: No, it _wasn't_.

1 A: When _____ the first World Cup?
  B: It _____ in 1930.
  A: _____ it in Greece?
  B: No, it _____. It _____ in Uruguay.

2 A: Who _____ the actors in *Casablanca*?
  B: They _____ Humphrey Bogart and Ingrid Bergman.
  A: And, in the film, _____ they in love?
  B: Yes, they _____, but they _____ married.

3 A: Where _____ the Olympic Games in 2000?
  B: They _____ in Sydney.
  A: How many different sports _____ there?
  B: There _____ 37, I think.

Get talking

8 **In groups, play 'The Memory Game'. Take turns to throw a coin and to ask and answer questions. Use the ideas to help you.**

Example:
A: Where was your best holiday?
B: It was in Tenerife.
C: Who were you with?
B: I was with my family.

Language to go

A: What was your favourite subject at school?
B: Well, it wasn't English or maths. It was sport!

> GRAMMAR REFERENCE PAGE 113
> PRACTICE PAGE 98

37

LESSON 18

Vocabulary   Everyday activities
Grammar   Past simple regular verbs (positive and negative)
Language to go   Talking about your week

A week in the life of ...?

Speaking and vocabulary

1 **Complete the sentences about the woman in the photo. Use the verbs in the box.**

> call   finish   study   talk   want to   start
> arrive   clean

1 I **study** Spanish in the morning because
   I _____ work in Spain.
2 I _____ my friends on my mobile and we meet
   for lunch.
3 I leave home at 3.30 p.m. and _____ work at
   4.00 p.m.
4 The theatre staff _____ at 5.00 p.m.
5 I _____ to people all night.
6 We close at 1.00 a.m. and we _____ the
   theatre.
7 I _____ work at 2.00 a.m. and take a taxi home.

2 **In pairs, describe a typical day for you. Use some of the verbs in Exercise 1.**

Reading

3 **Read the article and decide if the statements are true (T) or false (F).**

1 Martine relaxed on Monday.   ☐
2 She talked to the American guests
   on Tuesday.   ☐
3 The new girl started work on
   Tuesday.   ☐
4 There was a show on Wednesday.   ☐
5 On Wednesday she finished work
   at 2 a.m.   ☐

A week in the life of ...
a theatre manager

by Martine Andrassi *(Manager of the Centre Theatre in Sydney)*

Monday Free at last! It was a busy weekend at work so I stayed in because the theatre was closed. I didn't want to go out so I cooked dinner and watched a movie on video.

Tuesday A busy day on the phone! I called New York about the MTV Music Awards. I asked the organisers about the numbers of American guests. Then I talked to the manager of Raffles Agency in Bondi about a new dressing room assistant.

Wednesday The music awards show – very busy all day! Imogen, the new dressing room assistant, arrived at 5.00 p.m. The Awards started at 7.30 p.m. and I think everything was OK. I didn't have time to talk to people and I didn't finish work until 3.00 a.m.

Grammar focus

4 Look at the examples of the past simple regular verbs and complete the rules.

I call**ed** New York.
The new girl arriv**ed**.
I **didn't have** time.

1 We make the past simple positive with infinitive + _____ .
2 We make the past simple negative with _____ + infinitive (without *to*).

Note: Look in the Phrasebook for a list of irregular verbs.

5 Look at the table of spelling rules and complete it.

Regular verb	Past simple
call	call**ed**
talk	_____
arriv**e**	arriv**ed**
dance	_____
stud**y**	stud**ied**
try	_____

6 a) 📼 **Look at the table. Listen to the pronunciation of *-ed* in the past simple.**

b) 📼 **Listen to more verbs and put them in the correct column.**

visit**ed**	call**ed**	watch**ed**

Practice

7 Look at the lists in Martine's diary and write complete sentences.

Thursday
finish work at 2 a.m. ✓
clean flat ✗
1 cook dinner ✗
2 call mother ✓
3 watch a movie ✗

Friday
1 study Spanish ✓
2 start work at 4 p.m. ✓
3 the new concert posters arrive ✗
4 talk to musicians ✓
5 finish work at 2 a.m. ✗

Thursday
Examples:
She finished work at 2 a.m.
She didn't clean her flat.

1 _____
2 _____
3 _____

Friday
1 _____
2 _____
3 _____
4 _____
5 _____

Get talking

8 Talk about what you did last week.

1 Think about what you did last week. Use the verbs in the box to help you.

cook	arrive	stay in	watch	call	want to
start	finish	clean	study	visit	work
talk	play				

2 Tell your group what you did. Find other students who did the same as you.

Example: **I cooked dinner for friends on Friday.**

Language to go

A: You watched TV all weekend!
B: No, I didn't. I studied English.

> GRAMMAR REFERENCE PAGE 113
> PRACTICE PAGE 98

Vocabulary	Common irregular verbs
Grammar	Past simple irregular verbs
Language to go	Telling a story

Love at first sight

Vocabulary and speaking

1 Write the letter of the picture next to the verb in the box below. Some of the verbs match with more than one picture.

meet someone **E** __	fall in love __ __
go to her house __	buy her flowers __
give presents __	say 'no' __
leave her house __	see him with her __

2 In groups, number the pictures in the correct order to tell the story.

Listening

3 🔊 Listen to the real life love story about Tom and Jane on the radio. Check your answers to Exercise 2.

Grammar focus

4 a) Look at these examples of verbs with irregular past simple forms.

Example: have → *had*
think → *thought*

Now look at the recording script on page 122 and write the irregular past simple of the verbs.

meet _____ give _____
fall _____ say _____
go _____ leave _____
buy _____ see _____
come _____

b) Look at the rule and complete the example.

We make the negative of the past simple with *didn't* + infinitive (without *to*).

Example: (see) He _____ _____ her.
(not He didn't saw her.)

Practice

5 Look at the picture on the right and complete the story about Violet. Use the correct form of the verbs in the boxes.

| go fall meet |

Violet **went** on holiday to Italy. She
(1)_____ a waiter called Giovanni at a local
restaurant and she (2)_____ in love instantly.

| be say think give come |

He (3)_____ very romantic and (4)_____
her flowers and (5)_____ he loved her. Violet
(6)_____ home two weeks later, but Giovanni
didn't come with her. She (7)_____ about him
every day.

| see go not love leave |

One month later she (8)_____ England and
went back to Italy. She (9)_____ to the
restaurant and (10)_____ Giovanni with
another woman. He (11)_____ Violet.

Get talking ...

6 In pairs, look at the pictures on page 40 again and retell the story. What happened to Jane next? Use the verbs in Exercise 1 to help you.

... and writing

7 Imagine you are Jane. Write a letter to a friend and tell him/her what happened.

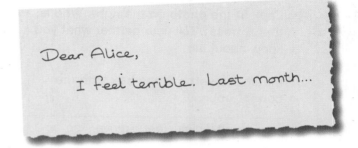

Dear Alice,
I feel terrible. Last month...

Language to go

I met him in the supermarket. We fell in love at first sight!

> GRAMMAR REFERENCE PAGE 114
> PRACTICE PAGE 99

LESSON 20

Vocabulary	Verbs and nouns: important events in life
Grammar	Past simple (questions)
Language to go	Asking questions to find out about people's lives

Life and times

Vocabulary and speaking

1 **Look at the photo on the right. Who is this actress? Tell your partner what you know about her.**

2 **Match the verbs in the box with the correct nouns.**

| be | start/finish | get | move | go |
| have | become | make | do | |

Example: <u>be</u> born, an actress, 30 years old

1 _____ married, a job, divorced
2 _____ to university, on holiday, abroad
3 _____ school, university, work
4 _____ house, flat, to the USA
5 _____ famous, an engineer, an actress
6 _____ a son, a daughter, a baby
7 _____ a film, a cup of coffee, money
8 _____ an English course, an exam, a driving test

Reading

3 **Read the article about Julia Roberts and match the dates to the events.**

1967   she got divorced
1984   she made her first film
1986   she moved to New York
1993   she was born
1995   she got married

All about ...
JULIA ROBERTS

● *Why is she famous?* American TV / cinema actress. Starred in *Pretty Woman*, *Notting Hill* and *Erin Brockovich*.

Grammar focus

4 **Look at these questions. Complete the table.**

Did she always *want* to be an actress?
No, she *didn't*. / Yes, she *did*.
When did she *get* her first job?
In 1984.

Question word	Auxiliary	Subject	Verb	Clause
✕	_____	she	want	to work with animals?
When	_____	she	make	her first film?

Practice

5 **Write the questions for the answers.**

Example: When <u>did she become an actress</u>?
        She became an actress when she was 17.

1 Who _____ for?
  She worked for 'Click' modelling agency.
2 _____?
  No, she didn't go to university.
3 When _____?
  She moved to New York in 1984.
4 _____?
  Yes, she got married to Lyle Lovett.
5 When _____?
  She got divorced in 1995.

STAR INTERVIEW

● *When was she born?*
Julia was born in Georgia, USA, in 1967.

● *Did she always want to be an actress?*
No, she didn't. She wanted to work with animals.

● *So, did she go to theatre school?*
Yes, she did. She left high school when she was 17 and started theatre school.

● *When did she get her first job?*
In 1984 she moved to New York and got a job as a model. She worked for 'Click' modelling agency.

● *What about love? Did she meet anyone special?*
She got married to Lyle Lovett in 1993 but, sadly, it didn't work. They got divorced two years later.

● *When did she make her first film?*
She acted in her first film, *Blood Red*, with her brother in 1986. She got her first Oscar nomination for *Steel Magnolias* when she was 22 years old. That was just the start ...

---

6 **a)** 🔊 **Listen to check your answers to Exercise 5.**

  b) Listen again and repeat.

7 **Ask your partner questions to complete the information about Kate Winslet.**

Student A: Turn to page 85.
Student B: Turn to page 88.

Get talking ...

8 **Interview your partner for an article about their life.**

  1 Prepare questions to ask your partner. Use the vocabulary in Exercise 1.
  2 Interview your partner.

... and writing

9 **Write an 'All about ...' article with the information from your interview.**

Language to go

A: When did you get married?
B: In 1983, 1989, 1993 and 1997!

> GRAMMAR REFERENCE PAGE 114
> PRACTICE PAGE 99

Vocabulary	Numbers
Grammar	Questions with *How* + adjective
Language to go	Asking for and giving measurements

Quiz show

Vocabulary and speaking

1 Write the numbers.

Example: five _5_

1 fifteen _____
2 twenty-five _____
3 fifty _____
4 one hundred _____
5 two hundred *and* five _____
6 two hundred *and* thirty-five _____
7 one thousand *and* fifty _____
8 one thousand, two hundred _____
9 seventy-five thousand _____
10 one hundred *and* five thousand _____

Note:
We write: 7.5 (not ~~7,5~~). We say: *seven point five.*
We write: 7,500. We say: *seven thousand, five hundred.*

2 📼 **Listen and repeat.**

3 📼 **Listen to the TV quiz show presenter. How much can you win for each question? Complete the list.**

4 Practise saying numbers.

Student A: Say the question number.
Student B: Say the prize money.

Example:
A: *Number 7.*
B: *£2,125.*

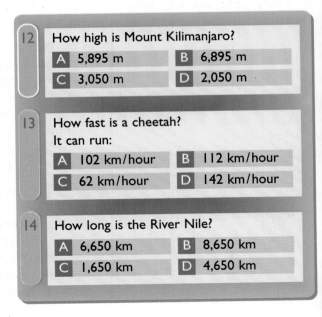

Win a Million!

1	_____
2	_____
3	£75
4	£100
5	£550
6	_____
7	£2,125
8	_____
9	£7,500
10	£14,000
11	_____
12	£51,000
13	£100,000
14	_____
15	£1,000,000

Listening

5 In pairs, look at the quiz questions and (circle) the correct answers.

12	How high is Mount Kilimanjaro?	
	A 5,895 m	B 6,895 m
	C 3,050 m	D 2,050 m

13	How fast is a cheetah? It can run:	
	A 102 km/hour	B 112 km/hour
	C 62 km/hour	D 142 km/hour

14	How long is the River Nile?	
	A 6,650 km	B 8,650 km
	C 1,650 km	D 4,650 km

6 📼 **Listen to the quiz show and check your answers to Exercise 5.**

Grammar focus

7 Look at the questions from the quiz show. Then look at the pictures and complete the questions 1–3 with the correct adjective from the box.

How high is Mount Kilamanjaro?
How fast is a cheetah?
How long is the River Nile?

fast

long
deep

high

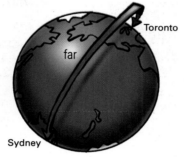
Toronto
far
Sydney
heavy

heavy	far	deep

1 How _____ is Cape Town from Cairo?
2 How _____ is an African elephant?
3 How _____ is Lake Baikal?

Practice

8 Make questions with *How ...?* to find out information about Canada and Australia.

Canada
1 Hudson Bay / deep?
2 CN Tower in Toronto / high?
3 Grizzly bear / fast?
4 Vancouver from Montreal / far?
5 Mackenzie River / long?

Australia
1 Uluru (Ayers Rock) / high?
2 Kangaroos / fast?
3 Murray River / long?
4 Sydney from Darwin / far?
5 Koala bears / heavy?

9 In pairs, use the questions from Exercise 8 to have a quiz.

Student A: Look at the information about Australia on page 85. Ask student B the questions in Exercise 8 about Canada and write down the answers.
Student B: Look at the information about Canada on page 88. Ask student A the questions in Exercise 8 about Australia and write down the answers.

Get writing ...

10 Prepare a television quiz.

Student A: Turn to page 85. Write the questions and three more possible answers for each question.
Student B: Turn to page 88. Write the questions and three more possible answers for each question.

... and talking

11 You are on a television quiz show.

Ask your partner your questions. How many did they get right?

Language to go

A: How far is the top of the mountain from here?
B: Only 3,429 metres.

> GRAMMAR REFERENCE PAGE 114
> PRACTICE PAGE 100

Vocabulary	Countable and uncountable nouns
Grammar	Expressions of quantity
Language to go	Talking about food you like

Sweet and savoury

Vocabulary and speaking

1 **In pairs, describe the photos of people's shopping. Use the words in the box.**

> chocolate biscuits crisps ice cream
> wine cakes bread butter coffee
> sweets cheese tomato ketchup cola

2 **Write the words from Exercise 1 in the table.**

Sweet	Savoury
chocolate	cheese

Listening

3 **Look at the photos of three shoppers. Guess which shopping basket belongs to each person.**

4 🔖 **Listen and write the number of the shopping basket next to each person.**

Lorraine ☐

Tim ☐

Melanie ☐

Grammar focus

5 **Look at the rules and write the words from Exercise 1 in the correct column in the table.**

Countable noun: we can count it – *one biscuit, two biscuits, ten biscuits.*
Uncountable noun: we can't count it – *some butter*
(**not** ~~one butter, ten butters~~).

Countable	Uncountable
biscuits	butter

6 **Look at the table and complete the rules below with *much, many*, or *a lot of*.**

How *many* cakes do you eat?	Do you buy *much* white wine?
Not many.	No, *not much.*
I don't eat *many* sweets.	I don't have *much* butter on my bread.

I buy *a lot of* crisps
She eats *a lot of* chocolate.
Yes, *a lot.*

1 We use _____ with countable nouns in questions and negatives.
2 We use _____ with uncountable nouns in questions and negatives.
3 We use _____ with countable and uncountable nouns in positive sentences.

Practice

7 **Underline the correct form in the sentences.**

Example:
A: How *much /* <u>*many*</u> biscuits do you eat?
B: Not *much /* <u>*many.*</u>

1 A: Do you eat *much / many* crisps?
  B: Not *much / many*. I like sweet things.

2 A: Do you eat *much / many* butter?
  B: No, but I eat *a lot of / many / much* bread.

3 A: Do you drink *much / many* cola?
  B: No, not *much / many*, but I drink
     a lot of / much / many coffee.

4 A: Are there *much / many* cakes in the cupboard?
  B: I don't know. There were *a lot / much / many* yesterday.

5 A: How *much / many* tomato ketchup do you put on your fish?
  B: *A lot / Much / Many*. I like ketchup.

6 A: There isn't *much / many* ice cream in the fridge.
  B: Really? How *much / many* did you eat last night?

Get talking

8 **Do the 'Sweet or Savoury?' questionnaire below.**

1 Complete the first column with the names of other foods.

2 Interview your partner and complete the questionnaire. Decide if they are a sweet or savoury person.

Example:
A: *Do you buy chocolate?*
B: *Yes.*
A: *How much chocolate do you buy?*
B: *Not much.*

SWEET OR SAVOURY?

Sweet	No	Yes	How much/many?
chocolate			

Savoury	No	Yes	How much/many?
cheese			

Language to go

A: Do you eat much chocolate?
B: Yes, a lot.

> GRAMMAR REFERENCE PAGE 114
> PRACTICE PAGE 100

LESSON 23

Vocabulary   Verbs and nouns describing changes in life
Grammar   *Going to* for future plans
Language to go   Talking about future plans

Big plans

Vocabulary and speaking

1   Complete the sentences about the couple in the photos with the correct form of the verbs in the box.

> earn   build   retire   change

1   At the moment, we _____ a lot of money as computer consultants.
2   We want to _____ our lifestyle and move from the city to the countryside.
3   We want to _____ a new house.
4   Our parents want to _____ to the countryside when they are 65.

2   Match the verbs on the left with the groups of words on the right.

1   to leave   a) weight, your wallet, money
2   to give up   b) to cook, to sing, to dance
3   to learn   c) to China, abroad, shopping
4   to go   d) school, university, a place
5   to lose   e) smoking, drinking, chocolate

3   Choose five things you want to do from Exercises 1 and 2. Tell your partner.

Reading

4   Read the article 'Stress free' about Simon and Emily. Answer the questions.

1   Did they live in the city or the country before?
2   Did they like it?
3   Do they live in the city or the country now?
4   Do they like it?

5   Complete the table about the differences between Simon and Emily's life in the city and in the country.

City	Country
successful job	no electricity

Grammar focus

6   a) Look at the sentences and complete the rule.

We *'re going to* build a house.
We *aren't going to* get stressed.

We use *am/is/are* + _____ _____ + infinitive to talk about future plans.

b) Complete the question forms for *going to*.

1   What _____ they _____ _____ do?
2   A: _____ you _____ _____ build a house?
    B: Yes, we are. / No, we aren't.

Simon and Emily Wilkinson, Atlanta, Georgia.

Stres

A successful job, lots of money, a beautiful flat in the city. Most of us dream of these things but for Emily and Simon of Atlanta, Georgia, all this was not enough. They had everything, but they weren't happy living in the city. They wanted to change their lifestyle so they gave up their jobs as computer consultants, left their house and bought some land in the Cumberland Mountains. Life is very different. There's no electricity, no shower for washing, no supermarket to buy food, but the husband and wife team love it and they have big plans.

So what are they going to do?

'First we're going to build a house. After that we're going to have lots of vegetables in the garden to eat.'

And are they going to work in the future?

'We're going to earn money by offering holidays to business people who need to escape the stress of the city, but this time we aren't going to get stressed.'

7   🔊 Listen and repeat.

learn English
to learn English
I'm going to learn English.

work
to work
aren't going to work
We aren't going to work.

ree

Practice

8   Complete the sentences about Simon and Emily's plans.

Example:
Emily and Simon / not change jobs again.
Emily and Simon aren't going to change jobs again.

1 What / they / do next year?
2 Emily / lose weight.
3 Simon / give up smoking.
4 They / not earn much money.
5 They / retire to the countryside.
6 They / go abroad?
7 They / not leave the Cumberland Mountains.
8 Emily / learn to cook meals for a lot of people.

Get talking

9   Talk about your plans.

1 Look at the notes. Tick (✓) the plans which are true for you. Add two more plans to each list.

Next two weeks	Next six months	Next five years
cook dinner	give up smoking	move house
do my homework	go abroad	get married
go to work	change my job	have a baby
go to a restaurant	buy new clothes	learn something new

2 In pairs, talk about your plans.

Example:
A: **Are you going to cook dinner next week?**
B: **Yes, but I'm not going to cook dinner every day!**

Language to go

A: Are you going to have children?
B: No, I'm not!

> GRAMMAR REFERENCE PAGE 114
> PRACTICE PAGE 101

Vocabulary Parts of a public building; American English
Grammar Prepositions of movement
Language to go Asking and giving directions

It's on the right

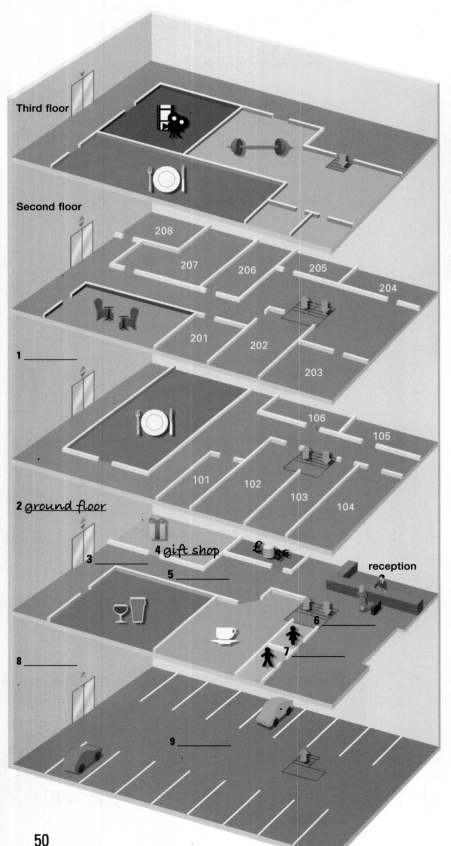

Third floor

Second floor

208
207   206   205
204
201   202   203
106   105
101   102   103   104

1 _____

2 *ground floor*

4 *gift shop*

reception

3 _____

5 _____

6 _____

7 _____

8 _____

9 _____

Vocabulary

1 **Write the words on the hotel plan.**

gift shop   car park   toilets
ground floor   lift   corridor
first floor   basement   stairs

2 **a) Look at these different British and American words.**

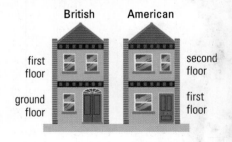

British   American

first floor   second floor
ground floor   first floor

b) Match the British and American words with the same meaning.

British	American
1 lift	a) movie theater
2 toilets	b) elevator
3 car park	c) hall
4 cinema	d) restroom
5 corridor	e) parking lot

Listening

3 📼 **Listen to a guest asking for directions at reception. <u>Underline</u> the correct answers.**

1 The guest wants to go to the
   restaurant / Red Lounge.
2 She takes the *stairs / lift.*
3 It is on the *first floor / second floor.*

Grammar focus

4 **Match the expressions below for giving directions with the pictures A–F.**

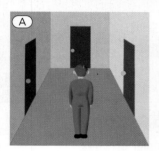

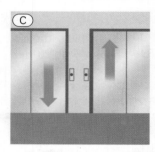
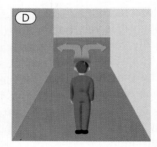

1 It's on the left/right/in front of you.   A
2 Turn left/right, …   __
3 Come out of the lift, …   __
4 Go along the corridor, …   __
5 Go up/down to the first floor, …   __
6 Go past the gift shop, …   __

Practice

5 **Look at the hotel plan and complete the directions from reception.**

1 A: Excuse me. Where's the restaurant?
  B: There are two, sir. The nearest one is on the first floor. Go _____ to the first floor, come _____ _____ the lift. Turn _____, go _____ the corridor and turn _____. You'll see it on the left.
  A: Thank you.

2 B: Can I help you?
  A: Is there a gym here?
  B: Yes, madam, it's on the third floor. Come out of the lift and turn _____. Go _____ the cinema and then turn _____. The gym is on the _____.

3 A: Where's the parking lot?
  B: Sorry, sir. Could you say that again?
  A: The parking lot.
  B: Oh, the car park. Yes, go _____ the gift shop and take the lift. Go _____ to the basement. Come _____ _____ the lift and you'll see it _____ _____ _____ you.

6 📼 **Now listen and check your answers.**

Get talking

7 **Ask and give directions in a hotel.**

Student A: Look at the hotel plan on page 86. You are at reception. Ask directions for the gift shop, gym, Red Lounge and Room 104 and write them on your map.
Student B: Look at the hotel plan on page 89. You are at reception. Ask directions for the swimming pool, bar, Green Lounge and restaurant and write them on your map.

8 **Choose two places in the building you are in now. Ask your partner for directions.**

Language to go

A: Excuse me, where's the restaurant?
B: Go up to the thirtieth floor and it's on the left.

> GRAMMAR REFERENCE PAGE 115
> PRACTICE PAGE 101

51

Vocabulary   Weather
Grammar   Linking words: *because, so, but, although*
Language to go   Describing climate and lifestyle

Hot and sunny

1

2

Vocabulary and speaking

1   **Look at photos 1–4 of Boston, USA. In pairs, describe the weather. Use the words in the box.**

it's cloudy   it's windy   it's sunny
it's raining   it's snowing   it's hot
it's cold   it's warm   it's freezing

2   **Say which photo is *winter, summer, spring* and *autumn* (*fall* in American English).**

   1   Do you have summer and winter, spring and autumn (fall) in your country?
   2   Which is your favourite season and why?

Reading

3   **Read the article 'City Breaks ... Boston'. Find three things you can do in summer and three things you can do in winter.**

4   **Say if you want to go to Boston in the summer or in the winter. Tell your partner.**

City Breaks ... Boston

A perfect weekend break in summer or winter.

Summer (June 21–Sept 20)

Although it is very hot in Boston in the summer, the city is usually very quiet because many Bostonians go to the beaches in Cape Cod or the lakes of Maine. Summer is also the time for festivals in the countryside, so don't miss the outdoor concerts, live jazz festivals and the 4 July celebrations. Wear T-shirts and shorts because it's usually 20–35°C.

Winter (Dec 21–Mar 20)

Winter is very cold in Boston, but it is only three months of the year. It snows in December and January so you can go skiing and snowboarding. In the evening you can watch American football on TV, sit in front of the fire and eat 'New England Clam Chowder', a delicious fish soup.

Grammar focus

5   **a) Look at the pairs of sentences.**

   Winter is cold *but* short.
   Although winter is cold, it's short.

   Is the meaning the same or different?

   You can go skiing in December *because* it snows.
   It snows in December, *so* you can go skiing.

   Is the meaning the same or different?

   b) Read the article again and <u>underline</u> examples of *but, although, because, so*.

Practice

6 Look at the sentences about Boston in the spring and autumn (fall) and <u>underline</u> the correct linking word.

Example: It's warm and sunny <u>but</u> / because / so sometimes it snows and rains.

1 The baseball season starts in spring *although / so / but* you can watch games at the Fenway Park stadium.
2 Take an umbrella *because / although /so* it rains a lot.
3 It's usually warm in spring *but / so / because* take a coat *because / so / although* sometimes it is windy.
4 *Although / So / But* it sometimes rains in autumn, people like walking in the mountains.
5 People wear sweaters *but / because / although* it starts to get cold.
6 *So / Because / Although* it is autumn, some days are hot *but / so / although* some people go to the beach.
7 The trees are very beautiful in autumn *because / so / but* people go to the countryside to take photos.

7 Complete the sentences about you.

Example: I love <u>spring</u> because <u>I start going to the beach</u>.

1 Although I like _____, I don't like _____ .
2 I don't like _____, so I _____ .
3 I don't mind _____ but I hate _____ .
4 I hate _____ because _____ .

Get talking ...

8 Talk about what you can do where you live.

1 People from an English-speaking country are coming to live and work in your area. In groups, describe the weather and what you can do in each season.
2 Present your ideas to the class.

... and writing

9 Write an e-mail to the English speakers coming to your area. Tell them about the climate and lifestyle.

Language to go

A: Does it rain a lot in summer?
B: No, but bring an umbrella because it's hot and sunny.

> GRAMMAR REFERENCE PAGE 115
> PRACTICE PAGE 102

53

Vocabulary	Dates
Grammar	Time prepositions: *in, on, at*
Language to go	Talking about memorable times

A new year

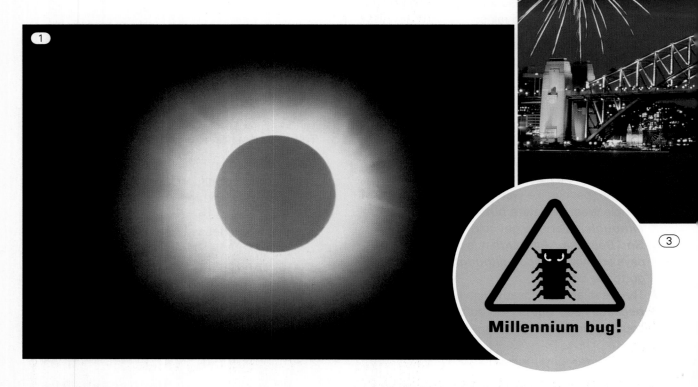

Vocabulary and speaking

1 **In pairs, look at the pictures of important events in 1999. What are the events? Do you remember them?**

2 **a) Look at the date on the photo:**

31-12-99

We say:
the 31st *of* December
December *the* 31st

We write:
31st December
December 31st
31/12/99 (UK)
12/31/99 (US)

b) Now say these dates.

3 🔊 **Listen and check your answers.**

Practice

7 Complete the sentences with *in*, *on*, or *at*.

Example: What happened *in* 1999?

1 My daughter was born _____ six o'clock _____ 1st January.
2 What did you do _____ December 31st?
3 I went to a party _____ the evening. It was brilliant.
4 I got married _____ February 14th, St Valentine's Day.
5 I started my new job _____ Monday, 21st October. I hate it.
6 I always go on holiday _____ August.
7 Did you move house _____ 2000?
8 What did you do _____ the weekend?

Get talking

8 Talk about important times in your life.

1 Think about five important times in your life and why they are important. Make notes.

Date	Event
June, 2001	left school

2 Tell your partner what you did and when.

Example: I *left school in June, 2001 ... I got married on January 1st.*

Listening

4 📼 **Listen to people talking on the radio about 1999. Write the number of the picture (in Exercise 1) next to the name of the caller.**

Dave ☐   Jennifer ☐   George ☐

5 Listen again and match the date on the left to the event on the right.

1 31/12/99
2 August 11th
3 November/ December

a) repairing computers
b) watched the fireworks in Sydney
c) saw the eclipse

Grammar focus

6 Look at the sentences and complete the headings in the table with *at*, *on* and *in*.

It was *on* Wednesday, *at* 11 o'clock *in* the morning.
We went to see the celebrations *on* 31st December.
In November and December, I spent most of my time in the office.

_____	_____	_____
November (months)	11th August	ten o'clock (time)
1999 (years)	(dates)	the weekend
the evening	Monday (days)	Christmas/Easter
	Christmas Day	lunch (mealtimes)

Language to go

A: When did you meet your wife?
B: At exactly 9.15 in the evening, on Monday, 21st August, 2000.

> GRAMMAR REFERENCE PAGE 115
> PRACTICE PAGE 102

Vocabulary   Everyday requests
Function   Permission and requests
Language to go   Asking for things and giving a response

Requests

Reading and speaking

Do our quiz and find out how polite you are.

HOW POLITE ARE YOU?

1 You want to use your friend's phone. What do you say?
a) Could I use your phone?
b) Where's the phone?

2 You can't hear what your friend says on the phone. What do you say?
a) Say again.
b) Could you say that again?

3 You want a taxi. What do you ask the hotel doorman?
a) I want a taxi.
b) Could you call a taxi, please?

4 How does the doorman reply to question 3?
a) Yes, of course.
b) Yes, I could.

5 You ask the hotel receptionist 'Could I pay by credit card?'. How does she reply?
a) No.
b) Sorry, I'm afraid we only accept cheques.

6 You ask a business client to tell you a good restaurant. What do you say?
a) Tell me about a good restaurant.
b) Could you recommend a good restaurant?

7 You're having dinner with friends and you want some salt. What do you say?
a) Could you pass the salt, please?
b) Salt, please.

8 You want a pen but you don't have one. What do you say to the waiter?
a) Could I borrow your pen?
b) Give me your pen.

Answers: Score one point for each correct answer.
1a, 2b, 3b, 4a, 5b, 6b, 7a, 8a.
1–3 = not polite 4–6 = polite 7–8 = very polite

---

1   Look at the pictures in the quiz 'How polite are you?'.

1 What do you think the people are saying?
2 Are you usually polite in these situations?
3 Are there any situations when you are not polite?

2   Do the quiz and compare your answers with your partner.

Vocabulary

3 **Underline the correct verb to use in each phrase. Look at the verbs in the quiz to help you.**

Example: _use_ / *take* the phone

1 *call* / *ask* a taxi
2 *demand* / *pass* the coffee
3 *tell* / *recommend* a good restaurant
4 *say* / *tell* something again
5 *pay* / *sell* by credit card
6 *call* / *borrow* your friend's car
7 *pay* / *accept* a cheque

Language focus

4 **Look at the requests from the quiz and complete the rules.**

Could I pay by credit card?
Sorry, I'm afraid we only accept cheques.
Could you call a taxi, please?
Yes, of course.

1 We use _____ + *I* + infinitive (without *to*) to ask for things.

2 We use _____ + _____ + infinitive (without *to*) to ask other people to do things.

3 To say 'Yes' we use *Yes, sure.* or _____ .

4 To say 'No' we use *Sorry,* and _____ and give a reason.

5 🔲 **Listen and repeat.**

1 A: Could you pass the coffee, please?
  B: Yes, of course.

2 A: Could I borrow your pen, please?
  B: Sorry, I'm using it.

3 A: Could you recommend a good restaurant?
  B: Yes, the Gold Star's not bad.
  A: OK, thanks.

4 A: Could I pay by cheque, please?
  B: Sorry. I'm afraid we don't accept cheques.

Practice

6 **Make the requests polite using *Could I ...?* or *Could you ...?***

Example: Give me your pen to use!
         Could I use your pen, please?

1 Pass the wine!
2 I want to borrow your car.
3 I want to pay and I've only got a credit card!
4 Say that again!
5 Tell me about a good restaurant.
6 I want to use your mobile phone.
7 Give me a coffee!
8 Tell me the way to the Tower Hotel.

7 **Match the answers to the questions in Exercise 6.**

a) Sure. Red or white?   _1_
b) Yes, I said my name is Sara.   __
c) Sorry, I'm new around here.   __
d) Yes, of course. Visa or Amex?   __
e) Sorry, I'm going to the airport so I need it. __
f) Yes, sure. Press the green button to call.   __
g) Yes. It's down this street on the left.   __
h) Yes, of course. Milk and sugar?   __

8 🔲 **Listen and check your answers to Exercises 6 and 7.**

Get talking ...

9 **Make some requests to your partner.**

Student A: Turn to page 86.
Student B: Turn to page 89.

... and writing

10 **Write a note to another student, making a request. The other student must write a note to answer you.**

Language to go

A: Could I pay by credit card?
B: Sorry, I'm afraid we don't accept cards.

> GRAMMAR REFERENCE PAGE 115
> PRACTICE PAGE 103

Vocabulary   Adjectives to describe places
Grammar   Comparatives
Language to go   Comparing places in your country

North and south

Vocabulary and speaking

1 **Look at the photos from New Zealand's North Island and South Island.**

   1 Is the north of your country different from the south? If so, how? Tell your partner.
   2 Do you want to live/work/study in the north or the south? Why? Why not?

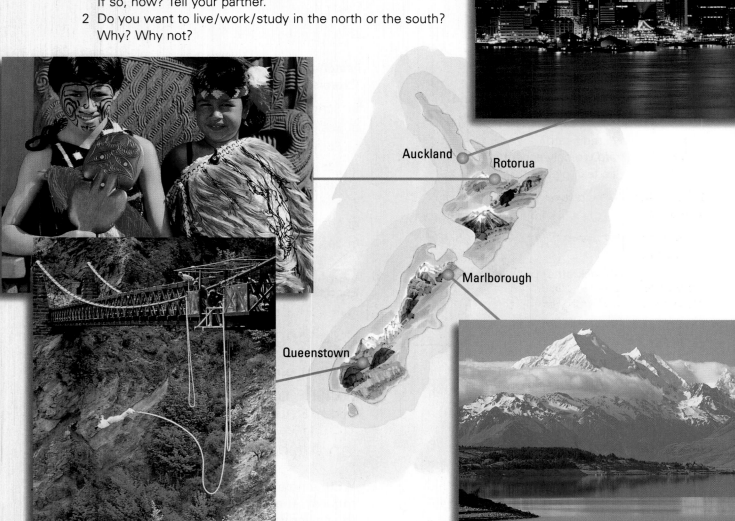

Auckland
Rotorua
Marlborough
Queenstown

2 **<u>Underline</u> the adjective which does not go with the noun.**

   Example: People: *friendly / interesting / <u>empty</u> / unfriendly*

   1 cities: *cosmopolitan / dangerous / historic / delicious / busy*
   2 weather: *hot / dirty / dry / wet / cold*
   3 beaches: *clean / dirty / crowded / empty / modern*
   4 countryside: *flat / small / quiet / beautiful / mountainous*

3 **In pairs, describe the pictures of New Zealand. Use the adjectives from Exercise 2.**

Listening

4 📼 **Listen to three people talk about their favourite place in New Zealand. Does each person talk about the North Island or the South Island? Write N or S.**

Speaker 1 ___
Speaker 2 ___
Speaker 3 ___

5 **Listen again and match the places on the left with the descriptions on the right.**

1 Auckland	a) dry, home of white wine, near mountains
2 Marlborough	b) wet, exciting, shops open seven days a week
3 Queenstown	c) modern, big, close to interesting historic places

Grammar focus

6 **Look at the sentences and complete the rules in the table.**

It's *bigger* and *more modern than* the other cities.
The climate is *drier*.
It's *wetter than* other places.
It's *more exciting than* other places.

	Adjective	Comparative
1 syllable	clean nice	clean*er* than nic*er*
Ends with 1 consonant + 1 vowel + 1 consonant	big flat wet	_____ flat*ter* than _____
Ends with 'y'	friendly dry dirty	friendl*ier* than _____ dirt*ier* than
2 syllables or more	cosmopolitan modern exciting mountainous	*more* cosmopolitan than _____ _____ *more* mountainous than
Irregular	good bad	*better* than *worse* than

7 📼 **Listen and repeat.**

bigger
bigger than
It's bigger than here.

more modern
more modern than
It's more modern than here.

Practice

8 **Complete the sentences.**

Example:
The south of Italy / hot / the north.
The south of Italy is hotter than the north.

1 Chicago / expensive / New Orleans.
2 New York / cosmopolitan / Dallas.
3 The south of France / dry / the north.
4 The north of Italy / wet / the south.
5 The south of Poland / mountainous / the north.
6 Brasilia / modern / Rio.
7 The north of Russia / cold / the south.
8 Holland / flat / Germany.

Get talking

9 **In groups, choose two places in your country to enter the 'City/Region of the Year' competition.**

1 Think about climate, people, countryside, food and drink, prices, free-time activities and culture.

2 Decide which place should win:
First Prize _____
Second Prize _____

3 Tell the class which city/region won the competition and why.

Language to go

A: Why do you think the north is better than the south?
B: Because I live there!

> GRAMMAR REFERENCE PAGE 116
> PRACTICE PAGE 103

Vocabulary   Adjectives to describe restaurants
Grammar   Superlatives
Language to go   Describing restaurants

The best food in town

Jumbo

busy

Solo per Due

comfortable

McDonald's

busy

Vocabulary

1   **Describe the restaurants with the adjectives in the box. Write the adjective under the photo.**

> famous   popular   comfortable   romantic
> friendly   busy   quiet   expensive   slow
> quick   old   small   big   cheap

2   **Put the adjectives from Exercise 1 in the correct column, according to the stress. Listen and check your answers.**

□	□□	□□□	□□□
slow			
quick			
old			
small			
big			
cheap			

Reading

3 **Read the reviews of the three restaurants and match them to the pictures in Exercise 1.**

1 _____

This place in Pushkin Square, Moscow, is the busiest and most popular fast food restaurant in the world. It's part of a chain of 57 restaurants in Russia which serve around 150,000 customers a day. Although they don't have the cheapest prices, they do have the quickest service. ■

2 _____

This is the smallest restaurant in the world. It has only one table and takes two people at a time. People come from all over the world to this 19th century villa to sit in front of the fire and enjoy the friendliest service, the best local food and wine and possibly the most romantic atmosphere of any restaurant in Italy.

3 _____

It is the biggest and the most famous restaurant in Hong Kong. Built in 1977, more than 30 million people have eaten at one of the 4,300 tables on the three boats. The oldest boat is called 'Tai Pak' and famous guests include John Wayne and Queen Elizabeth II. Here you can choose from over 100 different seafood dishes.

Grammar focus

4 **Complete the table. Find the superlative forms in the restaurant reviews in Exercise 3.**

	Adjective	Superlative
1 syllable	old	*the* old*est*
	small	_____
	quick	_____
	cheap	_____
	big	_____
Ends with 'y'	noisy	*the* nois*iest*
	busy	_____
	friendly	_____
2 syllables or more	comfortable	*the most* comfortable
	famous	_____
	romantic	_____
	popular	_____
Irregular	good	_____
	bad	*the worst*

Practice

5 **Complete the conversation. Use the adjectives in brackets in the superlative form.**

Example: Which is <u>the worst</u> (bad) restaurant in town?

A: Where is (1) _____ (good) restaurant to go on a Saturday night?
B: Well, (2) _____ (famous) is Arzak. The food is good but it's expensive.
A: What about the new French café in the square?
B: That's definitely (3) _____ (romantic) place but it's also (4) _____ (expensive). How much money do you want to spend?
A: Not that much. Where's (5) _____ (cheap) good place in town?
B: How about Hua? It's (6) _____ (popular) Chinese restaurant in town. It's not (7) _____ (comfortable) but it's definitely (8) _____ (busy) on a Saturday night.

6 **In pairs, look at the table and compare three restaurants.**

Example:
Hua has the friendliest service.

	HUA	ROMA	BURGER HOUSE
Friendly service	5	4	4
Quick service	4	2	5
Food quality	4	5	3
Atmosphere	3	4	2
Price	$$$	$$$$$	$

(1 = bad, 5 = excellent)

Get talking

7 **Look at the photos of the restaurants again. In groups, decide which one to go to and give your reasons.**

Language to go

A: Where's the nearest place to eat?
B: That restaurant there, but it's also the worst.

> GRAMMAR REFERENCE PAGE 116
> PRACTICE PAGE 104

On the phone

Vocabulary and speaking

1 Match the words in the box with the photos A–E.

> pager ___
> text message ___
> area code ___
> answering machine ___
> mobile phone (UK)/cellphone (US) __A__

2 Complete the sentences.

> text   take a message   put you on hold
> call you back   leave a message
> Directory Enquiries (UK)/Information (US)

Example:
> Sue isn't in. Do you want to **leave a message**?

1
> Is that _____?
> I need to find a number.

2
> I'll _____ while I check if Mr King is in the office today.

3
> Sorry, John's out.
> Can I _____?

4
> If I _____ her, she can phone me later.

5
> Sorry, Kate's having a bath.
> Can she _____ later?

3 In pairs, discuss the questions.

1 Do you like answering machines/voicemail? Why? Why not?
2 Do you like leaving messages? Why? Why not?
3 Do you have a mobile phone? Do you text people?

Reading

4 Read the advice on using telephones.

Write the headings *Answering* and *Calling* in the correct place (above 1–4 or 5–8).

Phone Etiquette

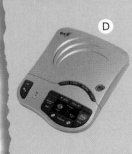
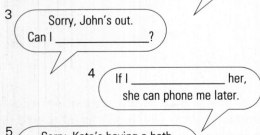

A

B

C

D

E

London 020
Edinburgh 0131

Everyone knows how to use the phone, right? Wrong. In today's world, phone skills are essential. 70% of communication is not what you say, but how you say it.

_____

1 Don't ring before 7 a.m. or after 9.30 / 10 p.m.

2 Say 'hello', give your name then ask for the person you want to speak to.

3 When you leave a message, give your name again and your number, if necessary.

4 Thank the other person at the end of the call.

_____

5 The correct way to answer is 'hello'. 'Yes' is rude.

6 The caller wants to speak to a person who is not there. Say 'sorry' and offer to take a message.

7 Repeat the caller's message to check it is correct.

8 Make sure you have the caller's number.

Listening

5 [🔊] **Listen to the telephone conversation and complete the message.**

> **Telephone message**
>
> Caller's Name: ....
>
> Message: Please call ☐ Person will call back ☐
>
> Number: ....

Language focus

6 **Look at the telephone conversation below. Write the number of the advice from Exercise 4 next to the telephone expressions. (You can use a number more than once.)**

_5_ Hello.
___ Hi, this is Tom. Can I speak to Sue?
___ Sorry, she isn't here at the moment. Can I take a message?
___ Yes, please. Could you ask her to call me back? It's Tom.
___ Call Tom. Has she got your number?
___ It's 01632 895506.
___ So that's 01632 895506.
___ Thanks very much. Bye.

Practice

7 <u>**Underline**</u> **the correct form.**

Example:
A: Can I speak to Emily?
B: Yes, _I am / **This is**_ Emily.

1 A: Can I speak to Pippa?
  B: Sorry, _she not / **she isn't**_ here at the moment.

2 A: Hello.
  B: Hi. _**This is** / I am_ Pete. Can I speak to Frances, please?

3 _Has she got / Has she_ your number?

4 A: Can I take a message?
  B: Yes, could you ask her to _call me back / call back me?_

8 **In pairs, have a conversation on the phone.**

1 Student A: Turn to page 86. Write what the caller says.
  Student B: Turn to page 89. Write what the person answering says.

2 In pairs, read your conversation. Student A calls, Student B answers.

Get talking

9 **In pairs, call your friend and leave a message.**

Hello. → Peter?
No! Out. Message? → Call me back.
Got number? → 0191 498 0004
0191 498 0004? → Goodbye.

Language to go

A: Can I speak to Pete, please?
B: This is Pete.

Vocabulary   Social etiquette
Grammar   *Should* for advice
Language to go   Giving advice to visitors

Culture shock

Vocabulary and speaking

1   **Match the phrases in the box with the pictures.**

> shake hands ___
> arrive on time __1__
> take your shoes off ___
> give a present ___
> kiss ___
> wear a suit ___
> bow ___
> use first names ___

2   **In pairs, describe the pictures. Which of these things do you do in your country?**

Listening

3   🎧 **Listen to a businesswoman give her Japanese colleagues advice on living and working in the UK or the USA. Tick (✓) the good ideas.**

1   Arrive on time. ☐
2   Use first names on first meeting. ☐
3   Take a present for a friend when you visit their house. ☐
4   Take your shoes off when you enter their house. ☐

Grammar focus

4   **Look at the sentences. Complete the rules.**

You *should arrive* on time.
You *shouldn't take* your shoes off.
Should we *bow*?
Yes, you *should.* / No, you *shouldn't*.

We use _____ + infinitive (without *to*) to say it's a good idea.
We use _____ + infinitive (without *to*) to say it's a bad idea.

5 📼 **Listen and mark the stressed words.**

☐   ☐
Example: Should I wear a suit?

1 Should I take a present?
2 Yes, you should.
3 Should you use first names?
4 No, you shouldn't.

6 Listen again and repeat.

Practice

7 Complete the quiz with *should* or *shouldn't* and ⃝circle⃝ the correct answers. Check your answers on page 86.

Culture Quiz

Should you talk about business at a meal in China?
a) Yes, you <u>should</u> .   b) No, you shouldn't.

1 Should you wear a suit and tie to meet a new client in Saudi Arabia?
a) No, you _____ .   b) Yes, you should.

2 _____ you give a Russian six flowers?
a) Yes, it's lucky.   b) No, it's unlucky.

3 Someone gives you a present in Japan. _____ you open it:
a) immediately?   b) later?

4 In Germany you _____ use your boss's first name because it is not polite.
a) True.   b) False.

5 _____ you use your right or left hand to accept a present in Muslim countries?
a) Right.   b) Left.

6 When you are invited for dinner at a friend's house in the UK, you _____ arrive more than 15 minutes late.
a) True.   b) False.

7 'You _____ have a meeting in room 4 because it is unlucky.' This statement is true in which country?
a) Mexico.   b) China.   c) Poland.

Get talking ...

8 Give advice to some foreign friends coming to visit your family.

1 Make notes.

Greeting / Saying hello:
You should...

Meetings:

Giving presents:

Clothes:

Eating:

2 Tell your group the advice you are going to give.
What advice is the same?
What advice is different?

... and writing

9 Write an e-mail to your friends giving your advice.

Language to go

A: Should I take a present?
B: No, you should give it to me!

> GRAMMAR REFERENCE PAGE 116
> PRACTICE PAGE 105

Vocabulary   Money verbs
Function   Suggestions
Language to go   Making suggestions for social arrangements

Party time!

Speaking and vocabulary

1   **In pairs, discuss the questions.**

1   What kind of party is in each photo?
   a birthday party ___
   a fancy dress party ___
   a leaving party ___
2   Do you like parties?
3   When did you last go to a leaving party
   or a fancy dress party?
4   How do you celebrate your birthday?

2   **Match the verbs on the left with the sentences on the right. Complete the sentences.**

1   buy

2   afford

3   pay

4   cost

5   rent

6   spend

a) The meal _____ £30.
   How much did it _____?
b) I'm going to **buy** a new dress for the party.
   I want to **buy** a present for you.
c) Can you _____ that dress? It's very expensive.
   I can't _____ to go out. I haven't got any money.
d) John's going to _____ for dinner on your birthday.
   He'll _____ by credit card.
e) I usually _____ a lot of money on clothes.
   We are going to _____ £500 on the party.
f) I want to _____ a car for the weekend.
   He's going to _____ a house in the countryside.

Listening

3 CD **Listen to a professional party organiser talking to a client from an advertising company. They are discussing an end-of-year party. Tick (✓) the things they talk about.**

drinks ☐	date of party ☐
place ☐	number of guests ☐
music ☐	food ☐

4 **Listen again and <u>underline</u> the correct answer.**

1 The party is at *the Sheraton Hotel / the office*.
2 They want to drink *champagne / wine*.
3 They want *karaoke / a DJ*.

Language focus

5 **Look at the expressions used for making suggestions.**

Suggestions

Shall we rent the room at the Sheraton?
Let's have it at the office.
How about having a fancy dress party?
How about the food and drink?

Responses

Well, we can't really afford it.
Yes, *that's a good idea.*
No, I'd rather have a smaller party this year.
Yes, the food was great last year *but ...*

6 a) CD **Listen and repeat.**

A: How about having a party?
B: Yes, that's a good idea.
A: Shall we have it at the office?
B: Let's have it in a nightclub.

b) **In pairs, practise the suggestions and answers.**

Practice

7 **<u>Underline</u> the correct expressions.**

1 A: Let's *going / go* out for dinner on your birthday.
  B: No, I'd rather *have / to have* a party.
  A: But we can't afford it.
  B: OK. How about *inviting / invite* some friends round for dinner?
  A: Yes, *that / that's* a good idea.

2 A: Shall we *having / have* a fancy dress party?
  B: No, I don't really like them.
  A: How about *getting / get* a DJ?
  B: Yes, that's a good idea.
  A: Let's *ask / to ask* James to do it.

8 **In pairs, practise the dialogues in Exercise 7.**

Get talking

9 **In groups, plan a leaving party for someone at work or college. You can afford to spend £500. Look at the costs below.**

PARTY PLANNER			Tick (✓) here
Location	At the office	£0	
	Hotel	£150	
Food	Snacks e.g. crisps, cheese, sandwiches	£75	
	Buffet	£150	
	Formal Dinner	£275	
Drinks	Champagne	£250	
	Beer	£75	
	Wine	£100	
	Soft drinks e.g. cola, juice	£50	
Music	DJ	£100	
	Karaoke	£50	
Entertainment	Photographer	£75	
	Games	£100	
	Celebrity guest	£300	
	Total:		

Language to go

A: It's your birthday. Let's have a party!
B: I'd rather have a present!

> GRAMMAR REFERENCE PAGE 116
> PRACTICE PAGE 105

LESSON **33**

Vocabulary   Movies
Grammar   *Say* and *tell*
Language to go   Talking about movies

At the movies

Vocabulary and speaking

1   **Match the film reviews to the photos.**

1 ___

'The best *romantic* film in the history of cinema. A classic black and white movie.'

2 ___

'Another fast and exciting *action* movie.'

3 ___

❝ Best science fiction film ever. ❞

4 ___

'It makes everyone laugh. A *comedy* for the family.'

2   **Say in which photos you can see:**

1 an *actor*   ___
2 an *actress*   ___
3 *special effects*   ___
4 mountain *scenery*   ___

3   **In pairs, discuss the questions. Use the vocabulary in Exercises 1 and 2.**

1 What type of film do you like?
2 Who's your favourite actor/actress?
3 What was the last film you saw at the cinema?
4 What's on at the cinema at the moment?

Reading

4   **Read the article about memorable moments in film history. Underline the correct answers to the questions.**

1 Which film does Mariana like?
  Star Wars / Casablanca.
2 Why? *The actor / The special effects*.
3 Which film does Magda like?
  Star Wars / Dr No.
4 Why? *The scenery / The actor*.
5 Which film does Tomás like?
  Dr No / Casablanca.
6 Why? *The story / The director*.

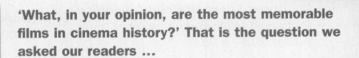

'What, in your opinion, are the most memorable films in cinema history?' That is the question we asked our readers ...

'I think *Star Wars* is one of the best science fiction films. The special effects are fantastic and the story is interesting. I can't remember the name of the actor but I love the scene when Luke fights Darth Vader.' **Mariana, Brazil**

'I love James Bond films and my favourite is *Dr No*. It was the first 007 movie and although the beginning is quite slow, the end is excellent. Sean Connery is the best James Bond actor and he always will be.' **Magda, Poland**

'One of my favourite films is *Casablanca* – I love old, romantic films. I think the story and the music are really good. Black and white films are my favourites.' **Tomás, Spain**

Grammar focus

5 **Look at the sentences. Then <u>underline</u> the correct words in the rules for *say* and *tell*.**

Mariana *said* she really *liked* Star Wars.
She *said that* she *loved* the special effects.
Tomás *told us* he *loved* Casablanca.
He *told us that* black and white films *were* his favourites.

1 There is no object after *say / tell*.
2 There is always an object after *say / tell*.
3 We use the *present / past* after *said* and *told*.

Practice

6 **Complete the sentences. Use the correct form of *say* or *tell*, and the verb in brackets.**

Example: Tomás <u>told</u> me that he <u>loved</u> (love) the music in *Casablanca*.

1 Magda _____ that she _____ (love) James Bond films.
2 She _____ me that Sean Connery _____ (be) a good actor.
3 She _____ that *Dr No* _____ (be) her favourite Bond film.
4 Tomás _____ us he _____ (like) black and white films.
5 He _____ his favourite film _____ (be) *Casablanca*.
6 Mariana _____ John that the special effects in *Star Wars* _____ (be) fantastic.

Get talking ...

7 **Make notes about your favourite films.**

Name of film:
Actor/Actress:
Director:
Special effects:
Music:
Scenery:
Story:

8 **Ask three people in your class about their favourite film. Then tell the others.**

... and writing

9 **Write a short review for your favourite film.**

Language to go

A: Steve said he liked James Bond because of the action.
B: He told *me* he liked James Bond because of the beautiful actresses!

> GRAMMAR REFERENCE PAGE 117
> PRACTICE PAGE 106

Vocabulary	Restaurant words
Grammar	*Would like/like, would prefer/prefer*
Language to go	Ordering food and drink in a restaurant

Would you like the menu?

2 Simple Salmon

Soup of the day

* * *

Salmon Ritz
Salmon Savoy
Salmon Plaza
Mixed salad
Mixed vegetables

* * *

Fruit salad
Selection of cheese

10% SERVICE CHARGE INCLUDED

3

RED	
House red	£8.00
Cabernet Sauvignon	£11.50
Rioja	£12.00
WHITE	
House white	£8.00
Soave	£11.00
Chardonnay	£12.50

Speaking and vocabulary

1 In pairs, ask and answer the questions.

1 How often do you go to restaurants?
2 What's your favourite restaurant? Why?

2 Describe the pictures above using the words in the box.

> salt pepper olives waiter customer
> menu wine list knife fork spoon
> wine glass

3 Look at the menu and the wine list. Complete the sentences using the words in the box.

> bill house red/white starter side dish
> dessert main course

Example: The soup is a **starter** .
1 The Salmon Ritz is a _____ .
2 The mixed salad is a _____ .
3 The fruit salad is a _____ .
4 When you pay the _____ , there is a 10% service charge.
5 The cheapest wine is the _____ .

Listening

4 🔊 **Look at the menu and wine list. Listen to two people ordering and tick (✓) the food and drink they want.**

5 **Listen again and match the name of the dish with the description.**

1 Salmon Ritz   a) salmon with tomato sauce, black olives and pepper

2 Salmon Savoy   b) salmon with pepper sauce, fresh tomatoes and olives

3 Salmon Plaza   c) salmon with green olive sauce, tomatoes and pepper

Grammar focus

6 **Look at the key. Write *a* or *b* next to the sentences.**

> Key:
> a = what you usually like
> b = what you want now/in the future

1 Do you prefer red or white wine?
   I prefer red wine.   *a*

2 Do you like olives?
   Yes, I do. I like black olives.   ____

3 Would you prefer mixed salad or vegetables?
   We'd prefer salad.   ____

4 What would you like?
   I'd like the Salmon Savoy.   ____

Note: *I'd like = I would like*
I'd prefer = I would prefer

Practice

7 a) 🔊 **Listen and tick (✓) the sentences you hear.**

1 a) I like some cheese. ☐
   b) I'd like some cheese. ☐

2 a) Do you like black coffee? ☐
   b) Would you like black coffee? ☐

3 a) I prefer red wine. ☐
   b) I'd prefer red wine. ☐

b) Listen again and repeat.

8 ⬭Circle the correct answers.

Example: Would you like to see the wine list?
    a) No, I don't like wine.
    ⬭b) No, thank you.

1 Do you prefer black or green olives?
   a) I'd prefer black.
   b) I prefer black.

2 Are you ready to order?
   a) Yes, I like soup for my starter.
   b) Yes, I'd like soup for my starter.

3 Would you like some coffee?
   a) Yes, I'd like an espresso.
   b) Yes, I love espresso.

4 Can I help you?
   a) Yes, I'd like a table for four.
   b) Yes, I like a table for four.

9 **Complete the restaurant conversation.**

Example: Table for two?
   Would you like a table for two?

A: Order?
B: Yes, the salmon.
A: Starter?
B: No.
A: What drink?
B: House white.
A: Dessert?
B: No. Bill, please.

Get talking

10 **You want to take your business/study colleague to dinner in a smart restaurant.**

Student A: You are a waiter/waitress.

Students B and C: You are customers in the restaurant. Use the menu on page 88.

> GRAMMAR REFERENCE PAGE 117
> PRACTICE PAGE 106

LESSON 35

Vocabulary Practical activities
Grammar Present perfect for experience
Language to go Asking people about their practical experience

Island life

Speaking and vocabulary

1 Look at the photo and tell your partner if you would like to live there.

2 Read part A of the 'Adventure TV' advertisement and answer the questions.

   1 What does the TV company want?
   2 Would you like to do this? Why/Why not?

3 Look at part B. Match the problems with the activities.

4 Look at part C. Match what they give you with the activities.

Reading

5 Read Andrew Ho's application form. Tick (✓) the correct boxes.

Name: Andrew Ho

Age: 34

1 Have you ever lived abroad?   YES ☐   NO ☐

Details: I've lived in Greece. I cooked for large groups in a hotel, and I went camping at the weekend. I think that the experience is useful for Mulkinney.

2 Have you ever taught children?   YES ☐   NO ☐

Details: I haven't, but I've taught adults. I don't think it's very different.

3 Have you had any experience with animals?   YES ☐   NO ☐

Details: I haven't worked on a farm but my family has had a lot of pets. I think I'm good at looking after animals.

ADVENTURE TV

A *Mulkinney is a North Atlantic island. Nobody lives there. We are looking for 30 people to survive on the island for a year. We want to see how people live when they are not in the modern world.*

B These are the problems you have on the island:

There are ...
1) no food shops
2) no houses
3) no schools
4) no clothes shops

So we need people to ...
a) build houses
b) grow vegetables
c) make clothes
d) teach children

C **We give you ...**
1) eight chickens and two cows
2) a laptop
3) a video camera
4) a guitar

So we need people to ...
a) play an instrument
b) use a video camera
c) look after animals
d) use a laptop

Grammar focus

6 a) Look at the sentences from the application form. Then answer the questions.

Have you ever *taught* children?
I'*ve taught* adults.
(I *have*)
I *haven't worked* on a farm.
(I *have not*)
My family *has had* a lot of pets.

1 Is he teaching adults now? *yes / no*
2 Do we know exactly when he taught adults?
   yes / no

b) Complete the rules for the present perfect.

1 We use the present perfect to talk about
   experience when the time *is / is not* important.
2 We make the present perfect with _____ or
   _____ + past participle.

Note: The past participle of regular verbs is: verb + -*ed*.
A list of the past participles of irregular verbs is in the
Phrasebook.

Practice

7 Complete the conversations with the correct form of the present perfect.

Example:
A: <u>Have</u> they ever <u>used</u> (use) a video camera?
B: Yes, they <u>have.</u>

1 A: _____ you ever _____ (write) a diary?
  B: Yes, I _____ .

2 A: _____ she ever _____ (teach)
     children?
  B: No, she _____ , but she _____
     (look after) her younger brother.

3 A: _____ they ever _____ (look after)
     animals?
  B: No, they _____ .

4 A: _____ you ever _____ (play) the
     piano?
  B: Yes, I _____ . I _____ (play) the guitar
     as well.

5 A: _____ he ever _____ (grow)
     vegetables?
  B: Yes, he _____ . He grows potatoes every
     year.

Get talking

8 Choose another person to go to Mulkinney.

1 Tick (✔) the activities on the form which you
  have done.
2 Interview two students in your class and tick
  (✔) the activities which they have done.

Example:
A: Have you ever grown vegetables?
B: Yes, I have.

	You	Student 1	Student 2
grow vegetables			
look after animals			
build a house			
teach children			
make your own clothes			
use a video camera			
write a diary			
go abroad			

Language to go

A: Have you ever made
   your own clothes?
B: Yes, I have.

> GRAMMAR REFERENCE PAGE 118
> PRACTICE PAGE 107

Vocabulary   Activities at work
Grammar   *Have to/don't have to*
Language to go   Describing jobs

Hard work

Vocabulary and speaking

1   **In pairs, discuss the question.**

What job would you like to do and why?

2   **Complete the job descriptions. Use the correct forms of the words in the boxes.**

drive to work   arrange meetings   work in a team

A personal assistant

I work in an office with five colleagues so we (1) _____ . My boss tells me who he needs to see and I phone clients to (2) _____ . Next year I'm going to get a company car so I can (3) _____ .

meet clients   travel   give presentations

A sales manager

I love my job because I (4) _____ to different countries. I use a laptop to (5) _____ to clients about the company. I enjoy talking to different people so I like (6) _____ .

make decisions   serve customers   work long hours

A shop assistant

I (7) _____ . I work from 8 a.m. to 8 p.m., six days a week. I (8) _____ and help them choose what clothes to buy and what size to get. I don't like my job because I can't (9) _____ – I just do what my boss tells me.

3   **In pairs, say which activities from Exercise 2 you do in your job, or want to do.**

Reading

4   **Look at the photo of a pizza delivery man and answer the questions.**

1   Which of the activities in Exercise 2 do you think he does in his work?

2   What other activities do you think Marcus does in his work?

5   **Read the article 'Nine to five' and check your answers to Exercise 4.**

PIZZA
To Go

Name: Marcus Willis
Job: Pizza delivery man
Wages: $6.00/hour

Nine to five

So you think my job is simple? You take the pizza from the shop, drive around town, go back to the shop and repeat. Unfortunately, it isn't that easy. I don't earn much per hour so I have to work long hours – sometimes I start at 3 p.m. and finish at 2 a.m. I drive about 80 miles a night and I have to use my own car because the company doesn't give me one. Another problem is the tips. Customers don't have to give me extra money, but with no tips I don't earn much. When I finish driving, I have to serve customers in the shop with the other workers. And my boss? Does he have to meet

Grammar focus

6 Look at the sentences from the article and <u>underline</u> the correct words in the rules.

I *have to work* long hours.
He *has to sit* in his office.
Does he *have to meet* the customers?
Yes, he *does*. No, he *doesn't*.
Customers *don't have to give* tips.

1 We use *have to* (or *has to*) + infinitive when something *is / isn't* necessary.

2 We use *don't/doesn't* (or *have to*) + infinitive when something *is / isn't* necessary.

7 [icon] Listen and repeat.

have to
have to serve customers
I have to serve customers.

have to
Does he have to
Does he have to meet clients?

the customers? No, he doesn't. He just has to sit in his office and answer the phone before he goes home at 6 p.m. After reading this, I hope you will be nice to the drivers who deliver pizza to your house!

Practice

8 Write complete sentences. Use the correct form of *have to*.

Example: What / do / in your job?
What do you have to do in your job?

1 We / meet clients.
2 I / not / serve customers.
3 What / your boss / do?
4 He / give presentations.
5 You / travel? Yes / do.
6 You / work in a team? No / not.
7 They / not / work long hours.
8 You / wear a suit?

Get talking

9 Look at the list of jobs and write one more you want to do. Complete the table with activities people *have to/don't have to* do in these jobs.

Do you want to be a ...?	Have to ...	Don't have to ...
shop assistant		
doctor		
politician		
personal assistant		
teacher		

10 In groups, order the jobs from 1–6 in order of preference. (1 = the best, 6 = the worst). Tell the other groups your reasons.

> GRAMMAR REFERENCE PAGE 118
> PRACTICE PAGE 107

LESSON 37

Vocabulary   Parts of the body; illnesses
Function   Making and accepting apologies
Language to go   Making excuses

Excuses, excuses

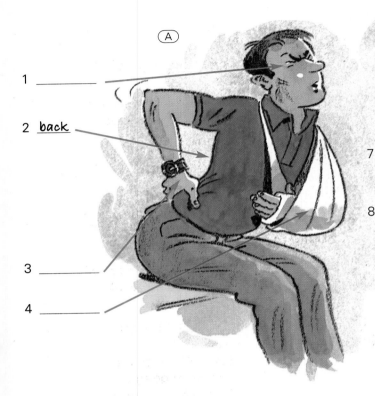

Ⓐ

1 _____

2

3 _____

4 _____

Ⓑ

5 _____

6 _____

7 _____

8 _____

Ⓒ

9 _____

10 _____

11 _____

12 _____

Vocabulary and speaking

1 Write the words in the box next to the parts of the body in the pictures.

| back | hand | foot | head | eye | arm | ear |
| throat | leg | stomach | nose | mouth | | |

2 In pairs, practise the words in Exercise 1.

Student A: Point to a part of the body.
Student B: Say the word.

3 Write the letter of the person in the picture next to the illnesses below.

Example: 'I've got a headache.' **B**

1 'I've got a sore throat.'   ____
2 'I've hurt my back.'   ____
3 'I've got a stomachache.'   ____
4 'I've got a temperature.'   ____
5 'I've hurt my arm.'   ____
6 'I've got a cold.'   ____
7 'I've got a cough.'   ____

4 🎧 Listen and tell your partner what the illness is.

5 Test your partner on the names of illnesses.

Student A: Point to a part of your body and mime an illness.
Student B: Say the illness.

Listening

6 🔊 **Listen to Tony tell his boss why he can't come to work. Put the excuses he gives in the correct order.**

___ He's got a cold.
___ He's hurt his back.
_1_ He's got a cough.
___ He's got stomachache.

Language focus

7 Look at the sentences and complete the table with the expressions in *italics*.

I'm (really) sorry, but I'm not feeling very well. *I've got a headache.*
Don't worry./That's OK.

I'm afraid I can't come to work. *I've got a temperature.*
What a pity!

Apology	Explanation	Accept apology
I'm (really) sorry, but		Don't worry!
	I've got a temperature.	

8 🔊 **Listen and repeat.**

sorry   cold
I'm sorry, but I've got a cold.
pity!
What a pity!

Practice

9 Match the apologies 1–5 to the responses a)–e).

1 I'm afraid I can't come to class because I'm not feeling very well.
2 I'm sorry, but the train was late.
3 I'm really sorry, but I've broken the plate.
4 I'm afraid I can't come to work today, I've got a temperature.
5 I'm sorry, but I can't play football today. I've hurt my leg.

a) What a pity! How did you hurt it? ___
b) That's OK. I'll tell you what we're going to do and you can study at home. _1_
c) Don't worry, it wasn't expensive. ___
d) That's OK, nobody else is here yet. ___
e) Don't worry! Take some aspirin and stay in bed. ___

Get talking

10 In pairs, make excuses.

Student A: Turn to page 86.
Student B: Turn to page 89.

Language to go

A: I'm afraid I can't come to work. I've got a sore throat and I can't speak.
B: What a pity!

> GRAMMAR REFERENCE PAGE 118
> PRACTICE PAGE 108

LESSON 38

Vocabulary   World issues
Grammar   *Will* for predictions
Language to go   Making predictions

Big issues

Vocabulary and speaking

1   **Match the words on the left to the examples on the right.**

1 Economy   a) United Kingdom – 56 million people
2 Transport   b) money, bank
3 Space   c) cloudy, rain, hot
4 Politics   d) car, aeroplane, bus
5 Population   e) the moon, Mars, a space station
6 Communication   f) phone, satellite, e-mail
7 Climate   g) government, president, The White House

2   **Match the words (1–7) in Exercise 1 to the photos.**

3   **a) Mark the stress on the words in the box.**

Example: technology □

> politics   transport   space
> climate   population
> economy   communication

b) 📼 **Listen to check your answers.**

4   **In pairs, discuss which of these things has changed the most in your lifetime.**

Reading

5   **Read Arthur C Clarke's predictions for the future. Which ones have already come true? Tell your partner.**

File   Edit   View   Favorites   Tools   Help

Back   Forward   Stop   Refresh   Home

Address Http//www.bravenewworld.com.uk

Brave New Wor

In 1967, the scientist Arthur C Clarke made these predictions abo the year 2000.

1 We will have satellite TV. Englis will become the main world langu used in satellite TV programmes.

2 We will have newspapers on computers. People won't use pape and we will get our information fr TV screens.

3 We will have e-mail around the world. People will have friends fro all over the world and not just in their own country.

38

Grammar focus

6 a) Look at the website in Exercise 5 and complete the sentences.

1 We _____ go on holiday in space.
2 People _____ live in cities.
3 What _____ happen in the future?

b) Now complete the rule.

We use _____ (*not*) + infinitive (without *to*) to make predictions about the future.

c) Look at these sentences and decide which is more natural – a) or b).

a) I think we won't have satellite television.
b) I don't think we'll have satellite television.

7 a) 🎧 Listen and tick (✓) the words you hear.

1 a) I will ☐   b) I'll ☐
2 a) I won't ☐   b) I want ☐
3 a) will ☐   b) we'll ☐
4 a) they ☐   b) they'll ☐

b) Listen again and repeat.

4 **People won't live in cities. They will live in small, independent communities in the countryside.**

5 **The population will increase to 6 billion and then will get smaller. By the end of the 21st century, only a few million people will live on Earth.**

6 **People won't work in offices. They will work at home and communicate with computers.**

7 **We will have automatic cars with no drivers. Cars won't use gasoline.**

8 **We will use technology to make healthier food.**

9 **We will go on holiday in space. There will be hotels on space stations as well as on the moon and Mars.**

Some of these have already come true. What will happen in the future? Please e-mail to predictions@newworld.com.uk

Practice

8 Complete the sentences about the year 2050.

Example:
The population of the world / not increase.
The population of the world won't increase.

1 Where / people / go on holiday?
2 I / not think / people / go on holiday in space.
3 You think / computers / listen to instructions?
4 I think / everyone / speak English.
5 The climate in the UK / not be hotter.
6 You think / technology / cost less?
7 I think / transport / be cheaper.
8 The world economy / be stronger.

Get talking

9 Make predictions for an Internet discussion group.

1 A website on the Internet asks you to send in predictions for the year 2050. In groups, discuss your predictions for the topics below.

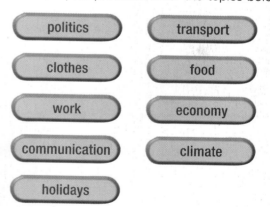

Example: *In 2050, people will work ten hours a week.*

2 Change groups and discuss your predictions.

> GRAMMAR REFERENCE PAGE 119
> PRACTICE PAGE 108

Vocabulary   Expressions of time with *for* and *since*

Grammar   Present perfect: *how long/for/since*

Language to go   Talking about how long people do things for

Long life

Speaking and vocabulary

1   **Look at the photos in the article. In pairs, discuss the questions.**

   1   How old are the people in the pictures?

   2   When you are their age, will you:
     – have a job?
     – live somewhere different?
     – study?

   3   What do you think you will you be interested in?

2   **Match an expression on the left with a similar expression on the right.**

   1   over ten years
   2   New Year's Day
   3   ages
   4   a couple of months
   5   midday

   a)   1st January
   b)   two months
   c)   twelve noon
   d)   more than ten years
   e)   a long time

3   **Say which expressions from Exercise 2 are:**

   1   a point in time
     Example: *twelve noon*

   2   a period of time
     Example: *two months*

Reading

4   **Read the newspaper article about the three women in the pictures. Match the women with their jobs and ages.**

Dodo	singer	70 years old
Carmen	tennis player	72 years old
Omara	model	86 years old

Life begins at 65!

Today, not all people over 65 think they're old. People stay younger for longer. Three women who are examples of this philosophy are Dodo, Carmen and Omara. What do they do and how long have they done it?

▲ Omara Portuondo

▲ Carmen Dell'Orefice
◄ Dodo Cheney

Dodo Cheney is an 86-year-old tennis champion. She has played tennis for more than 70 years. Now she plays in competitions for people over 75 and she has won over 285 matches – more than Pete Sampras.

Carmen Dell'Orefice is 70 years old and she has been a model since she was 13. Her career started 57 years ago when a photographer saw her on a bus and asked to take her photo. Today she still works for the Ford modelling agency.

Cuban singer **Omara Portuondo** is one of the most popular jazz singers in the world. She has sung in clubs and cabarets for over 50 years and was on the 'Buena Vista Social Club' album. Now she is 72 years old and is still one of the star singers at the famous Tropicana Club in Havana, Cuba.

Grammar focus

5 a) Look at the examples and answer the questions.

She *has played* tennis for 70 years.

1 When did she start playing tennis?
2 Does she play tennis now?

We use the present perfect for actions that started in the past and continue now.

Note: *She's played* is the contracted form of *She has played*.

b) Underline two more examples of the present perfect in the text.

c) Look at the questions and answers. Complete the rules with *for* or *since*.

How long has Dodo played tennis?
For more than 70 years.
How long has Carmen been a model?
Since she was 13.

1 We use _____ with a period of time.
2 We use _____ with a point in time.

Practice

6 Write sentences using the present perfect and *for* or *since*.

Example: She started playing tennis 70 years ago. She plays tennis now.
She's played tennis for 70 years.

1 He started teaching football 48 years ago. He teaches football now.

2 I started playing jazz in 1950. I play jazz now.

3 I have a dog. I bought him in 2001.

4 He started dancing when he was twelve. He dances now.

5 She paints. She started painting two years ago.

6 She started a new job on 10 January. She works there now.

7 We started English lessons last year. We study English now.

8 They live in Australia. They moved there eight years ago.

Get talking ...

7 Look at the table. How long have you done these things for?

1 Complete the table about yourself.

2 Interview your partner and complete the table.
   Example:
   A: *Where do you live?*
   B: *Madrid.*
   A: *How long have you lived there?*
   B: *Since 1998.*

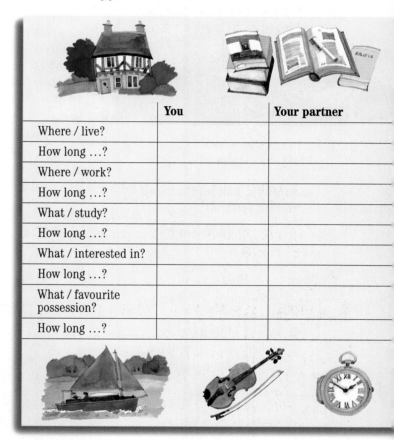

	You	Your partner
Where / live?		
How long ...?		
Where / work?		
How long ...?		
What / study?		
How long ...?		
What / interested in?		
How long ...?		
What / favourite possession?		
How long ...?		

... and writing

8 Use the table to write an article about your partner.

Language to go

A: How long have you been married?
B: For two months!

> GRAMMAR REFERENCE PAGE 119
> PRACTICE PAGE 109

Vocabulary   Work
Function   Giving opinions, agreeing and disagreeing
Language to go   Discussing what makes a good job

The perfect job

Family lunches, beds and bars...

Employees don't want just high salaries every year and pensions when they retire. Now they want to enjoy work. So, bosses are making it more fun to go to the office than stay at home:

■ British Airways has got its own village with a shopping centre, cafés, a supermarket and a gym for employees.

■ Saatchi & Saatchi has got a pub where colleagues can have a beer at work.

■ Somerfield supermarket have even got an Internet dating agency so that their employees can find love in the office!

■ Other companies have crèches for young children, sofas, flowers and games rooms to make the workplace more like home.

Speaking

1   **In pairs, ask and answer the questions.**

1   Are the people in the photos at home or at work?
2   Would you like to work/study in a place like this?
3   Which of these things would you like to have at work/college/school?

Reading

2   **Read the article and match the words in the box to the companies.**

café   dating agency
gym   supermarket   pub
shopping centre

1   British Airways (an airline):
   café

2   Somerfield (a supermarket):
   _____

3   Saatchi & Saatchi
   (an advertising agency):
   _____

Vocabulary

3   **Match the words from the article to the definitions.**

1   an employee   a) a person you work with
2   a salary   b) a place for children aged 0–5
3   a pension   c) an organisation (for example, British Airways)
4   a boss   d) a person who works for a company
5   a colleague   e) money you get after you retire (in old age)
6   a company   f) money you earn from working
7   a crèche   g) a manager (informal)

Listening

4 🎧 **Listen to a manager and a psychologist talk about what employees want at work. Who talks about the things below? Write M for *Manager* or P for *Psychologist*.**

1 sofa, café, crèche ☐
2 dating agency ☐
3 high salary ☐
4 friendly colleagues ☐
5 good boss ☐

Language focus

5 **Write these headings at the side of the table.**

> Asking for opinion   Disagreeing
> Giving opinion   Agreeing

Asking for opinion	What do you think? Do you agree?
	In my opinion … I think … (people work hard) I don't think …
	That's true. Yeah. Yes, I agree.
	No, I don't think so. Yes, … but (some companies are doing too much). No, I disagree. I don't agree.

Practice

6 **Complete the dialogues with expressions from Exercise 5.**

1 A: _I think_ a bar at work is expensive for the company.
  B: Yes, _____ colleagues sometimes have good ideas when they have a drink together.

2 A: In _____ _____ employees want a high salary.
  B: _____ true. Money is very important to some people.

3 A: I don't _____ working for an international company is very important.
  B: _____ _____ agree. I think people like working for big companies because they usually get a better pension.

4 A: I think people want long holidays. Do you _____?
  B: No, _____ _____ _____ _____.
  I think they want more money.

5 A: I _____ a comfortable work environment is important. _____ do you _____ ?
  B: I agree.

6 A: Money is more important than a good boss.
  B: No, I _____ . Money isn't everything.

Get talking

7 **Talk about conditions at work. Your boss wants to know what his/her employees want.**

1 Look at the list and choose the five most important things for you.
2 Number them (1–5) in order of importance and think about your reasons.
  1 = very important   5 = less important
3 In groups discuss your ideas. Agree on the top five and number them in order of importance.

How important is:	Your ideas	Group ideas
a good boss?	☐	☐
a bar?	☐	☐
a high salary?	☐	☐
an international company?	☐	☐
a pension?	☐	☐
a crèche?	☐	☐
a gym?	☐	☐
How important are:		
long holidays?	☐	☐
good colleagues?	☐	☐
Other:	☐	☐

Language to go

A: I think a gym at work is a good idea.
B: I agree!

> GRAMMAR REFERENCE PAGE 119
> PRACTICE PAGE 109

Lesson 3, Exercise 8, Group A

Use this information to write your quiz.

Leisure and Entertainment
Chess is Indian.
Samba and Bossa Nova are Brazilian.

Food and Drink
Guinness is Irish.
Pitta bread and kebabs are Turkish.

Famous People
Astérix and Obélix are French.
André Agassi is American.

Lesson 5, Exercise 8, Student A

Read the information about Rami from Syria.
Complete the sentences with the correct form of the
verbs. Then tell Student B about Rami's day.

get up   drink   eat   cook

Rami's special day is Eid.
We _____ at five in the morning.
We _____ special sweets in the morning.
My mother _____ lunch.
We _____ special coffee in the afternoon.

Lesson 10, Exercise 9, Student A

Lesson 11, Exercise 8, Student A

Lesson 14, Exercise 9, Student A

The Cormack family

Lesson 15, Exercise 9, Student A

You are a waiter/waitress. Your teacher will give you one of the menus below.

①
The Vegetarian Café

Sandwiches: cheese (with lettuce)	$3.00
Extra: tomato	$0.60
Cake: chocolate	$3.25
Cold Drinks: cola	$1.50
Fruit: apple	$1.75

②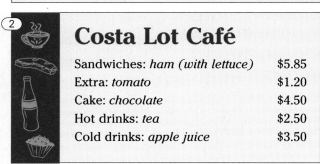
Costa Lot Café

Sandwiches: *ham (with lettuce)*	$5.85
Extra: *tomato*	$1.20
Cake: *chocolate*	$4.50
Hot drinks: *tea*	$2.50
Cold drinks: *apple juice*	$3.50

③
Jo's Snackbar

Sandwiches: chicken (with lettuce)	$2.00
Hot drinks: coffee	$0.65
Cold drinks: cola, juice	$1.00
Fruit: apple/banana	$1.00

Lesson 20, Exercise 7, Student A

Write the questions for 1–3 about Kate Winslet. Ask Student B your questions. Student B will ask you questions 4–6. Answer, using the information you have.

Kate Winslet
Questions:
1 When / have / first baby? _____ ?
2 When / start theatre school? _____ ?
3 Go abroad in 1984? _____ ?
Information:
4 London / age 11
5 no university
6 met husband / Morocco

Lesson 21, Exercise 9, Student A

Information about Australia
Uluru (Ayers Rock) is 868 m high.
Kangaroos can move at 48 km/hour.
The Murray River is 2,600 km long.
It is 3,157 km from Sydney to Darwin.
Male koala bears are between 8 and 14 kg.

Lesson 21, Exercise 10, Student A

Write the quiz questions. Make three more possible answers for each of the questions. Ask Student B your questions. How many did they get right?

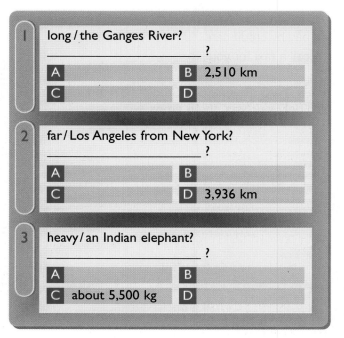

Lesson 24, Exercise 7, Student A

You are at reception. Ask Student B directions for:

- the gift shop
- the gym
- the Red Lounge
- Room 104

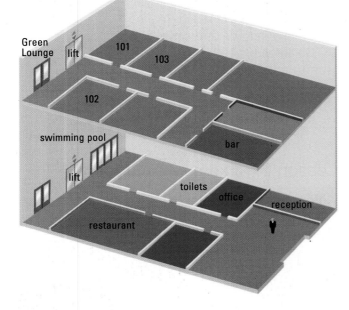

Lesson 27, Exercise 9, Student A

PART ONE Ask Student B for the following:

- recommend a good restaurant
- use their mobile phone
- borrow their pencil
- pay by credit card
- call a taxi for you

PART TWO Respond to Student B's requests. You can only say 'yes' three times.

Lesson 30, Exercise 8, Student A

Write what the caller says in the conversation on the phone.

B: Hello.
A: _____
B: Sorry, he isn't in at the moment. Can I take a message?
A: _____
B: Has he got your number?
A: _____
B: So, that's 570983.
A: _____
B: No problem. Bye.

Lesson 37, Exercise 10, Student A

Make these phone calls to Student B and make excuses.

A1 You've got a headache and you don't want to go to work. Phone your boss.

A2 You want to watch a football match tonight but your boyfriend/girlfriend wants you to go to the cinema. Phone him/her and make an excuse.

A3 Your manager wants you to go out for dinner with a client, but you want to go to your best friend's party. Phone your manager and make an excuse.

Answer these phone calls from Student B.

B1 You're an English teacher. A student phones to say they can't come to your English class.

B2 You're a manager and your employee calls to say they cannot come to an important meeting.

B3 Your friend phones to say they cannot help you move house.

Lesson 31, Exercise 7

Culture quiz
Key: 1b 2b 3b 4a 5a 6a 7b

Lesson 3, Exercise 8, Group B

Use this information to write your quiz.

Leisure and Entertainment
Sumo is Japanese.
Roulette is French.

Food and Drink
Sauerkraut is German.
Cognac and Champagne are French.

Famous People
Madonna is American.
Mick Jagger is British.

Lesson 5, Exercise 8, Student B

Read the information about Charlene from Jamaica.
Complete the sentences with the correct form of the
verbs. Then tell Student A about Charlene's day.

eat   listen   get up   drink

Charlene's special day is Independence Day.
We _____ at seven in the morning.
We _____ a fruit called *ackee* and saltfish for
breakfast.
My father _____ white rum.
I _____ to the music in the street.

Lesson 10, Exercise 9, Student B

£10
£40
£60
£15
£100
£175
£65
£30

Lesson 11, Exercise 8, Student B

Lesson 14, Exercise 9, Student B

The Cormack family

Lesson 15, Exercise 9, Student B

You are a customer. Your teacher will give you one of the cards below.

1 **Food:** cheese and lettuce sandwich **Drink:** orange juice	5 **Food:** cheese, lettuce and tomato sandwich a banana
2 **Food:** chicken and lettuce sandwich chocolate cake	6 **Food:** ham, lettuce and tomato sandwich **Drink:** cola
3 **Food:** ham and lettuce sandwich **Drink:** coffee with cream	7 **Food:** chicken, lettuce and tomato sandwich **Drink:** tea with lemon

Lesson 20, Exercise 7, Student B

Student A will ask you questions 1–3 about Kate Winslet. Answer, using the information you have. Write the questions for 4–6 and ask Student A your questions.

Kate Winslet
Information:
1 first baby / in 2000
2 theatre school / in 1986
3 yes/ the US / in 1984
Questions:
4 When / move / London? _____ ?
5 Go to university? _____ ?
6 Where / meet / husband? _____ ?

Lesson 21, Exercise 9, Student B

Information about Canada
Hudson Bay is 128 m deep.
The CN Tower in Toronto is 535 m high.
A grizzly bear can run at 56 km/hour.
It is 3,694 km from Vancouver to Montreal.
The Mackenzie River is 4,000 km long.

Lesson 21, Exercise 10, Student B

Write the quiz questions. Make three more possible answers for each of the questions. Ask Student A your questions. How many did they get right?

Lesson 34, Exercise 10, Students B and C

Starters	Soup of the day Tuna salad
Main course	Steak and chips Spaghetti Carbonara Chicken in white wine sauce
Side dishes	Green salad Greek salad Mixed vegetables
Dessert	Fruit salad Selection of cheeses

Lesson 24, Exercise 7, Student B

Look at the hotel plan below. You are at reception.
Ask Student A directions for:

- the swimming pool
- the bar
- the Green Lounge
- the restaurant

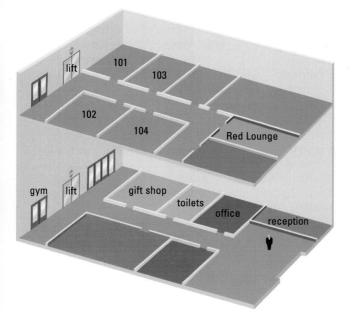

Lesson 37, Exercise 10, Student B

Answer these phone calls from Student A.

A1 You're a manager and your employee phones you because they are ill.

A2 Your boyfriend/girlfriend phones to say they cannot go with you to the cinema tonight.

A3 You're a manager. Your employee phones to say they cannot have dinner with an important client.

Make these phone calls to Student A and make excuses.

B1 You can't go to your English class because you have a temperature. Phone your teacher.

B2 You want to buy a cheap flight but it leaves on the same day as an important meeting at work. Phone to make an excuse not to go to the meeting.

B3 Your friend wants you to help them move house but you don't want to. Phone and make an excuse.

Lesson 27, Exercise 9, Student B

PART ONE Respond to Student A's requests. You can only say 'yes' three times.

PART TWO Ask Student A for the following:

- recommend a good hotel
- use their computer
- borrow their car
- book some cinema tickets for you
- pass a dictionary

Lesson 30, Exercise 8, Student B

Write what the person answering the phone says.

B: _____
A: Hi, this is Tom. Can I speak to Matthew, please?
B: _____
A: Yes, could you ask him to call me back?
B: _____
A: No. It's 570983.
B: _____
A: Thanks. Bye.

Lesson 1, Exercise 3

Practice

1 Meeting people

Vocabulary: personal information

1 Match the greetings with the responses.

1 Hello!	___	a) Fine thanks.
2 Nice to meet you!	___	b) Bye.
3 How are you?	___	c) And you.
4 Goodbye.	_1_	d) Hi!

2 Find ten more 'personal information' words (three jobs, three countries, three hobbies and one more word for marital status).

C	V	G	U	O	P	S	C	U	I	P	A
E	R	M	U	Q	Z	U	O	D	R	O	L
F	M	U	S	I	C	O	A	D	N	L	M
S	A	X	A	U	I	Q	W	A	F	A	O
G	R	H	J	X	S	T	U	D	E	N	T
I	R	U	V	B	M	E	A	O	N	D	P
S	I	N	G	L	E	Y	R	C	Y	T	F
Y	E	R	P	Q	E	J	L	T	R	U	I
F	D	S	C	B	N	S	P	O	R	T	L
P	A	B	R	A	Z	I	L	R	Y	O	M
S	D	C	V	R	T	H	O	P	S	Z	S
B	U	S	I	N	E	S	S	M	A	N	X

Grammar: *to be: am, is, are*

3 Underline the correct form.

P: Hi! My name **'m / 's / 're** Paola. (1) I **'m / 's / 're** married to Juan and we have three children. Here's a photo. (2) Jorge **'m / 's / 're** a doctor and (3) Isabella and Arantxa **'m / 's / are** students. (4) They **'m / 's / 're** interested in music and (5) I **'m / 's / 're** interested in learning English. And you?

M: Nice to meet you, Paola. (6) I **'m / 's / 're** Marek and this is my friend, Javel. (7) We **'m / 's / 're** from Poland. (8) I **'m / 's / 're** a doctor and (9) Javel **'m / 's / 're** a businessman.

2 Personal details, please!

Vocabulary: everyday objects

1 Underline the word which is different.

Example: dictionary   wallet   briefcase

1 notebook	diary	pen
2 laptop	calculator	bag
3 bag	briefcase	watch
4 laptop	mobile phone	pen
5 camera	wallet	bag
6 dictionary	diary	camera

Grammar: plurals; *What is/are ...?*

2 Write the plurals of these words in the table.

watch notebook   mobile phone   laptop   camera bag   battery   briefcase   diary   calculator   pen wallet   dictionary

-s	-ies	-es
cameras		

3 Look at the answers and write the questions.

Example:
A: <u>What's your telephone number?</u>
B: My work number is 7492 1598.

1 A: _____ ?
  B: My name's Barnard.
2 A: _____ ?
  B: M P.
3 A: _____ ?
  B: My first names? Matthew Peter.
4 A: _____ ?
  B: CA13 4XV.
5 A: _____ ?
  B: 3, Bridge Street, Cambridge.
6 A: _____ ?
  B: I'm a businessman. I work for an IT company.
7 A: _____ ?
  B: MPB@alloallo.com.uk

3 Round the world

Vocabulary: nationalities and countries

1 Complete the sentences with the correct country or nationality.

Example: Is he **British** ? (from the UK)

1 I'm _ _ _ _ _. (from Ireland)
2 Are you from _ _ _ _ _ _? (French)
3 I'm _ _ _ _ _ _ _ _. (from the USA)
4 They're _ _ _ _ _ _ _ _ _ _ _ . (from Argentina)
5 I'm not Polish, I'm _ _ _ _ _ _ _ . (from Russia)
6 We're _ _ _ _ _ _ _ _. (from Japan)

Grammar: *to be* (questions and negatives)

2 Read the information about Carmen and Mehmet and correct the sentences about them.

Name	Carmen Diaz Garmendia
Nationality	Spanish
Job	Doctor
E-mail address	Diaz10@santandina.com
Age	55
Married	Yes (José: doctor)
Interested in	Films, sport

Name	Mehmet
Nationality	Turkish
Job	English student
E-mail address	Met39@warmail.com.uk
Age	29
Married	No
Interested in	Music, sport

Example: Carmen ~~is~~ a student. ✗ **isn't**

1 Carmen and her husband aren't doctors.
2 Mehmet is a businessman.
3 Carmen isn't married.
4 Mehmet and Carmen are interested in books.
5 Carmen and Mehmet are French.

3 Complete the dialogue with the verb *be*.

M: Carmen, **are** you from Spain?
C: Yes, I (1) _____ . Where (2) _____ you from?
M: I (3) _____ Turkish, from Istanbul.
C: Mehmet, what (4) _____ you interested in?
M: Music. And you? (5) _____ you married?
C: Yes, I (6) _____ . My husband (7) _____ a doctor. What (8) _____ your job?
M: I (9) _____ an English student.

4 Favourite things

Vocabulary: free time activities

1 Complete the crossword.

Across
1 You go to a _____ to see beautiful old objects. (6)
5 *Language to go* is a _____. (4)
6 For example: tennis, football. (5)
8 You watch a _____ on TV. (9)
9 You can go to a street _____ to buy food and clothes. (6)

Down
2 Harrods is a famous British _____. (4)
3 For example: *Hello, Marie Claire, Vogue*. (8)
4 For example: *The Times, The Herald Tribune*. (9)
5 You go to a _____ to drink beer or whisky. (5)
7 *Casablanca* is a famous _____. (4)

Grammar: possessive adjectives and possessive *'s*

2 Complete the sentences with these words.

| her their our your their 's his |
| my 's its 's his |

Example:
A: Is that Julian's car?
B: Yes, **his** car is the blue one.

1 What's David _____ favourite sport?
2 A: I like English food but it is not _____ favourite.
  B: What 's _____ favourite food? French?
3 I like REM. _____ music is really good.
4 A: We live in the UK but _____ children are at university in the USA.
  B: Yes, _____ favourite city is Seattle.
5 A: Is Paul _____ sister an artist?
  B: Yes, she is. _____ pictures are in the Tate Gallery.
6 A: What's John _____ favourite restaurant?
  B: _____ favourite is Bella Napoli. _____ pizzas are excellent.

5 Celebrations

Vocabulary: activities: verbs and nouns

1 Underline the word in each group which doesn't match the verb.

Example: cook   *dinner / food / ice cream*

1 dance   *salsa / with someone / an instrument*
2 eat   *sushi / water / pizza*
3 play   *a present / cards / a game*
4 go   *for a walk / to bed / to music*
5 give   *money / for a walk / a present*
6 visit   *to bed / your family / a friend*
7 get up   *in the morning / at 10 a.m. / to bed*
8 drink   *beer / water / ice cream*

Grammar: present simple (positive)

2 Complete the sentences about the weekend with the correct form of these verbs.

| cook   eat   drink   go   visit   dance |
| get   go   play |

Example: I _cook_ dinner every night.

1 On Sunday mornings she _____ for a walk in the country.
2 On Saturdays we _____ football.
3 My parents _____ to the market on Sundays.
4 At the weekend, she _____ up at twelve o'clock.
5 They _____ salsa on Friday evenings.
6 I _____ my family every month.
7 My sister _____ sushi all the time.
8 He _____ wine at the weekend.

3 Look at the pictures of Jess and Pete's Christmas and complete the sentences.

On Christmas Day, after breakfast, we _give_ our presents to each other.

I (1) _____ lunch in the morning. At about three o'clock we (2) _____ lunch with my parents.

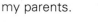

In the evening Jess, my girlfriend, (3) _____ TV and I (4) _____ cards with my parents. We (5) _____ to bed at about eleven o'clock.

6 The modern world

Vocabulary: activities: verbs and nouns

1 Underline the verb which goes with the nouns.

Example: _use_ / *do* the Internet and the phone.

1 *meet / buy* books and food
2 *meet / book* new friends
3 *speak to / buy* your doctor and your friends
4 *use / book* a hotel and a holiday
5 *listen to / do* an English course
6 *have / buy* a bank account and a credit card
7 *speak to / listen to* music

Grammar: present simple (questions and negatives)

2 Make the sentences negative.

Example: We use the Internet every day.
   We don't use the Internet every day.

1 I buy new books on the Internet.

_____

2 Nicole speaks to her friends by e-mail.

_____

3 She meets new friends in Internet chat rooms.

_____

4 They listen to music in cafés.

_____

5 Ryan has a bank account on the phone.

_____

6 He books holidays in a travel agent's.

_____

7 I want to do an English course on the Internet.

_____

8 Jim does a computing course with a private teacher.

_____

3 Insert the missing word.

Example: _Do_
   ⌐ you use the Internet?

1 they book hotels on the Internet?

2 he do a German course with a private teacher?

3 When you speak to your friends?

4 Marianna meet new friends at school?

5 Where you meet people?

6 What they buy on the Internet?

7 Trevor buy music in a shop or on the Internet?

8 Sarah and Nicky study French?

7 Travelling

Vocabulary: objects you take on holiday; means of transport

1 Find the transport words.

Example: inart   *train*

1 rac	_____	5 uwbyas	_____
2 xiat	_____	6 oabt	_____
3 yclbice	_____	7 nelpa	_____
4 ramt	_____	8 sub	_____

2 Write a list of the items in the pictures. Use *a*, *an* or *some* before the word.

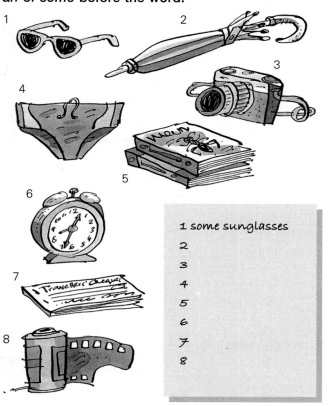

1 some sunglasses

2

3

4

5

6

7

8

Grammar: *a/an, some/any*

3 Complete the dialogue with *a*, *an*, *some* or *any*.

Example: Do you have **an** alarm clock?

A: So, you are going to Scotland next week. Do you have (1) _____ walking boots?
B: Yes, I do.
A: Do you have (2) _____ sweaters?
B: Yes.
A: Don't buy (3) _____ umbrella because you can take mine.
B: Oh, thank you.
A: It's a good idea to take (4) _____ camera. Do you have (5) _____ maps?
B: Three! I'm going to buy (6) _____ guide books when I get there.

8 The collectors

Vocabulary: objects that people collect

1 Circle the correct definition.

Example:
A book for photographs.   a) photo album
                          b) pictures

1 You drink out of them.   a) mugs   b) plates
2 Children play with them.   a) ornaments   b) toys
3 Artists paint them.   a) posters   b) pictures
4 You can wear this.   a) a T-shirt   b) a poster

Grammar: *have got*

2 Write two sentences about each picture using the correct form of *have got*.

Example: He/toy: **He's got a toy.**
            He/book: **He hasn't got a book.**

1 He/book: _____
  He/newspaper: _____
2 She/mug: _____
  She/plate: _____
3 They/poster: _____
  They/photo album: _____

3 Complete the questions with the verb *have got*.

Example: He / any photo albums?
         Has he got any photo albums?

1 Joanne / a poster of Brad Pitt?
_____
2 You / a favourite mug?
_____
3 Marie and Paul / any collections?
_____
4 They / a car?
_____
5 He / a big house?
_____
6 She / any ornaments?
_____

9 Top sports

Vocabulary: sports

1 Find eleven more sports.

S	W	I	M	M	I	N	G	W	V	L
A	K	S	K	I	I	N	G	A	O	C
B	A	S	K	E	T	B	A	L	L	Y
I	R	N	A	E	E	L	I	K	L	C
L	A	G	T	A	N	A	N	I	E	L
L	T	I	G	O	N	O	G	N	Y	I
A	E	R	O	B	I	C	S	G	B	N
I	O	L	L	S	S	D	O	C	A	G
N	A	E	F	O	O	T	B	A	L	L
G	J	O	G	G	I	N	G	J	L	W

2 Write the sports from Exercise 1 in the correct column in the table.

Use a ball	No ball
tennis	jogging

Grammar: verbs + –ing

3 Look at the information about Tara and Steven and write sentences about what they like/don't like. Use the verbs go, do or play.

	Tara	Steven
Love	skiing	karate
Like	aerobics	volleyball
Not mind	swimming	football
Not like	jogging	basketball
Hate	golf	cycling

Example: _Tara loves going skiing._

1 Tara _____ .

2 Tara _____ .

3 Tara _____ .

4 Tara _____ .

5 Steven _____ .

6 Steven _____ .

7 Steven _____ .

8 Steven _____ .

9 Steven _____ .

10 Shopping

Vocabulary: clothes

1 Find the clothes words.

Example: ritsh __shirt__

1 uoserrts _____
2 kitrs _____
3 srotsh _____
4 retaews _____
5 ketjac _____
6 itsu _____
7 rinserta _____
8 eshos _____
9 otobs _____
10 atoc _____

Function: asking for information in a shop

2 Put the words in the correct order.

Example:
1 you I help can?
Can I help you?

2 green have in you it got? _____ ?

3 you are size what? _____ ?

4 it can on try I? _____ ?

5 it much is how? _____ ?

3 Match the questions in Exercise 2 to these answers.

___ a) Yes, the changing room's over there.

___ b) I'm a size twelve.

___ c) It's $80.

___ d) No. We've only got it in black.

_1_ e) Yes. I like this shirt.

11 Interesting places

Vocabulary: adjectives to describe places in a town

1 Write the opposite of the adjectives.

Example:
This restaurant is very ~~busy~~ at the weekend. *X quiet*

1 The clothes in Guccio are very cheap. A shirt costs over £50.
2 People in cities like London are very friendly and never talk to you.
3 I think English food is bad.
4 My house is very quiet at the weekends. There are lots of people.
5 There's a really boring film on at the cinema. Do you want go?
6 That watch looks cheap. How much is it?
7 His English is very good so talk slowly.

Grammar: *there is/are*

2 Look at the map of this town and write sentences about it.

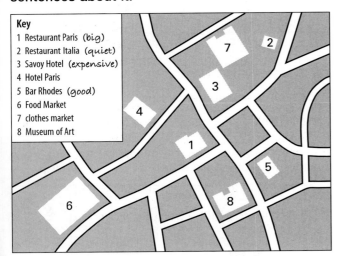

Key
1 Restaurant Paris (big)
2 Restaurant Italia (quiet)
3 Savoy Hotel (expensive)
4 Hotel Paris
5 Bar Rhodes (good)
6 Food Market
7 clothes market
8 Museum of Art

Example: restaurants
There are some restaurants.

1 museum?
_____

2 big restaurant
_____

3 good bar
_____

4 cinema
_____

5 hotels?
_____

6 markets
_____

12 The weekend

Vocabulary: everyday activities

1 Complete the conversations. Match the sentences 1–8 with the responses a)–h).

1 Jane wants to watch that film on TV.
2 Do you want to go for a drink?
3 I get a takeaway every Friday.
4 How often do you go to the gym?
5 On Saturdays I go to the beach.
6 I want to stay in.
7 In my office, we always work late.
8 I often meet my friends in the centre of town.

___ a) Good idea. I don't want to go out again.
___ b) When I want some exercise.
_1_ c) What channel is it on?
___ d) Fish and chips or Chinese?
___ e) And do your friends usually arrive on time?
___ f) Do you go swimming in the sea?
___ g) What time do you get home from the office?
___ h) OK. Look, there's a bar over there.

Grammar: adverbs of frequency

2 Put the words in the correct order.

Example: never we go beach to on the Mondays.
We never go to the beach on Mondays.

1 often do how stay you in?
_____

2 you takeaway sometimes do get a?
_____

3 no get a never I takeaway.
_____

4 am always I late.
_____

5 it busy is often?
_____

6 usually meet Sundays on friends they.
_____

3 Insert the adverb in the correct place.

Example: It is /always busy on Friday. (always)

1 I meet my friends at about nine o'clock. (usually)

2 I go to the gym. (never)

3 He works late several times a week. (often)

4 I am happy to get a takeaway. (always)

5 They are quiet after school. (often)

6 My family stays in once a week. (usually)

13 Office … or living room?

Vocabulary: furniture in an office/living room

1 Look at the picture and find eleven more items from the office in the word square.

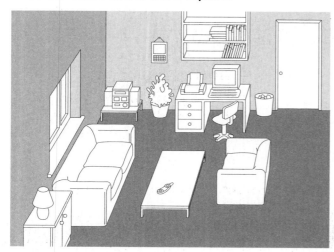

S	B	O	U	G	X	Y	D	L	O	O	X
M	B	K	S	T	E	R	E	O	V	M	N
M	O	Q	D	E	S	K	W	F	O	C	B
S	G	E	P	L	A	N	T	V	F	O	B
O	C	O	C	E	A	X	K	C	T	Q	C
F	P	C	U	P	B	O	A	R	D	J	X
A	R	M	C	H	A	I	R	Q	U	Q	Z
W	Y	B	O	O	K	C	A	S	E	L	A
N	P	R	I	N	T	E	R	Z	F	A	E
V	C	A	L	E	N	D	A	R	R	M	S
Q	D	B	I	N	Z	Y	M	X	P	P	Q
M	W	Q	U	C	Y	O	C	W	J	H	J

Grammar: prepositions of place

2 Look at the picture of the office and complete the sentences with these words.

on opposite above on next to in under in front of next to on

Example: The telephone's _on_ the table.

1 I've got a sofa _____ the window.
2 There's a table _____ the sofa.
3 I've got a computer _____ the room.
4 There's a bin _____ the door.
5 I've got the printer _____ the desk.
6 There's a calendar _____ a plant.
7 The armchair's _____ the sofa.
8 There's a lamp _____ the cupboard.
9 I've got the printer _____ the computer.

14 Family

Vocabulary: family

1 Put these words in the correct category.

brother father aunt grandfather daughter children husband son wife sister parents mother uncle grandmother

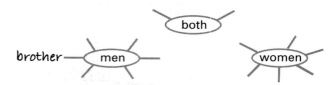

Grammar: present continuous for now

2 Complete the table with the -ing form or infinitive.

dance	dancing	sit	_____
watch	_____		having
_____	talking	go	_____
get	_____	swim	_____
study	_____		doing
_____	using	play	_____
give	_____	smoke	_____

3 Complete the sentences using these verbs.

take drink sit wear stand talk stand

Example: This is a photo of my family. I'm standing next to my brother and sister.

1 The woman on the left is my mother. Look, she _____ a glass of champagne.
2 My brother and sister _____ next to me.
3 That's my grandfather. He _____ a suit and he _____ to someone on his mobile phone.
4 My grandparents _____ next to my mother.
5 My father isn't here – he _____ the photo.

15 In a café

Vocabulary: food and drink

1 Circle the odd word out in each part of the menu.

Menu	Hot drinks	Fruit
	coffee	apple
	tea	banana
	cola	cheese
	chocolate	lemon
Sandwiches	**Cold drinks**	**Cake**
chicken	milk	chocolate
cheese	chicken	banana
tea (circled)	juice	tomato
tomato	chocolate	lemon

Function: making requests

2 Rewrite the sentences.

Example:
Can we have two teas with lemon?
(will) *We'll have two teas with lemon, please.*

1 Can I have a chicken sandwich?
(will) _____
2 Can I take your order now?
(will) _____
3 We'll have two large coffees, please.
(can) _____
4 I'll have an apple, please.
(can) _____
5 Can the children have cola?
(will) _____
6 I'll have a cheese sandwich with extra tomato.
(can) _____

3 Complete the conversations in a café.

1 A: *Are you* ready to order?
   B: Yes, _____ a chicken sandwich with no tomato.
   A: _____ else?
   B: _____ have a large cola?
2 A: Good morning, _____ a tea, please?
   B: _____ you are.
   A: _____ is that?
   B: $1.75.
3 A: I _____ the chocolate cake, please.
   B: Is that all?
   A: No, _____ an apple too, please?

16 Job skills

Vocabulary: activities at work

1 Tick (✓) the nouns which go with the verbs.

	a song	a car	people	a letter
to type				✓
to sing				
to manage				
to repair				
to design				
to drive				

Grammar: can for ability

2 Look at the information and complete the sentences using can/can't + verb.

	Felix	Sabrina
drive a car	✓	✗
read a map	✗	✓
design a website	✗	✗
manage a company	✓	✓
type 60 words per minute	✗	✓
speak a foreign language	✗	✓
repair a computer	✗	✗

Example: Felix *can drive* a car.

1 Sabrina _____ a car.
2 Sabrina _____ a map.
3 They _____ a company.
4 They _____ a website.
5 Felix _____ 60 words per minute, but Sabrina _____.
6 Felix _____ a foreign language.
7 They _____ a computer.

3 Complete the questions and answers.

Example:
A: *Can you speak* a foreign language?
B: Yes, I can. French and German.

1 A: _____ a car?
   B: No, I can't. I ride a bicycle.
2 A: Can she play an instrument?
   B: Yes, _____. She plays the piano.
3 A: _____ football?
   B: No, he can't. He's really bad at ball games.
4 A: _____ a website?
   B: Yes, they can. They love computers.
5 A: Can he read a map?
   B: No, _____. He always gets lost.

17 Memories

Vocabulary: question words

1 Complete the question words.

Example: W<u>hen</u> was your first English lesson?

1 W_____ is your English teacher?
2 W_____ is your English school?
3 H_____ o_____ are you?
4 H _____ m_____ people are in your English class?
5 H_____ m_____ is your coursebook?
6 W_____ are you interested in?

2 Match the questions in Exercise 1 to these answers.

___ a) $11.50.
___ b) I'm twenty.
___ c) Oxford, England.
_1_ d) Mrs Robinson.
___ e) Studying English.
___ f) Sixteen.

Grammar: past simple of *be: was, were*

3 <u>Underline</u> the correct form of the verb *be*.

1 A: Where <u>was</u> / *were* your best holiday?
  B: It (1) *was* / *were* in Greece five years ago. I (2) *was* / *were* with my boyfriend and we (3) *was* / *were* very happy.

2 A: When (1) *was* / *were* your first English lesson?
  B: It (2) *was* / *were* in 1999. There (3) *was* / *were* twelve people in my class and my teacher (4) *was* / *were* Australian.

3 A: Who (1) *was* / *were* your best friends at school?
  B: Gemma and Paula. There (2) *was* / *were* a group of girls at school and Gemma (3) *was* / *were* the first one to talk to me. We (4) *was* / *were* good friends then and are still good friends now.

4 Rewrite the sentences in the past simple.

Example:
Who is your English teacher?
Who was your English teacher?

1 My school is in Scotland.

_____

2 My friends aren't on holiday.

_____

3 They are at work.

_____

4 I am good at cycling.

_____

5 What are you interested in?

_____

18 A week in the life of ...?

Vocabulary: everyday activities

1 Match the verbs with the nouns.

1 to call   a) the house
2 to want to   b) English
3 to start/finish c) do something
4 to arrive   d) work at six o'clock
5 to clean   e) to a friend
6 to talk   f) at the cinema on time
7 to study   g) a friend

Grammar: past simple regular verbs (positive and negative)

2 Write the negative form of the sentences.

Example: He arrived at the party late.
  He didn't arrive at the party late.

1 We wanted to go to university.

_____

2 Lessons started at 8:30 in the morning.

_____

3 My friends studied French.

_____

4 Tony watched French films.

_____

5 I played football every Wednesday.

_____

3 Complete the letter using the past simple.

Dear Aunt Chrissie,
    I <u>arrived</u> (arrive) in Cambridge last Monday and it is excellent. My degree course (1) _____ (start) on Tuesday.
    I (2) _____ (stay) in on Wednesday night and (3) _____ (cook) dinner for a friend. We (4) _____ (not study) – we (5) _____ (talk) about the course.
    On Thursday I (6) _____ (watch) some friends play football. I (7) _____ (not play) because I (8) _____ (not have) my boots.
    On Friday I (9) _____ (not want) to stay in so I (10) _____ (visit) some other people on my course. We went to a nightclub but I (11) _____ (not dance) – you know me!
    I (12) _____ (call) you last night but you weren't at home. Speak to you soon.
    Love,
    Martin

19 Love at first sight

Vocabulary: common irregular verbs

1 Complete the verb table.

Infinitive	Past simple	Infinitive	Past simple
to go	*went*	_____	did
to have	_____	_____	left
_____	came	to see	_____
_____	said	to fall	_____
to think	_____	to meet	_____
to buy	_____	to give	_____

2 Match the beginnings with the ends.

1 My friends came   a) me a present.
2 Ian gave   b) on holiday in France.
3 I fell   c) about it for a long time.
4 We went   d) to my party.
5 I met   e) 'thank you'.
6 I thought   f) in love with him.
7 He said   g) some beautiful flowers.
8 She bought   h) some lovely people.

Grammar: past simple irregular verbs

3 Look at the pictures of Stephanie yesterday. Correct the sentences to make them true.

Example:
She ~~left~~ home at 7.30. ✗
didn't leave

1 She didn't go to work.

1 She didn't go to work.

2 She didn't drink a cup of coffee.

3 She ate a sandwich at work.

4 She didn't meet Ann at lunch time.

5 She bought some flowers.

6 In the evening they went to a restaurant.

7 She didn't give Eve a present.

20 Life and times

Vocabulary: verbs and nouns: important events in life

1 Complete the crossword.

1 to _____ an actress (6)
2 to _____ house (4)
3 to _____ a course (2)
4 to _____ a new job (5)
5 to _____ a cup of coffee (4)
6 to _____ a child (4)
7 to _____ married (3)

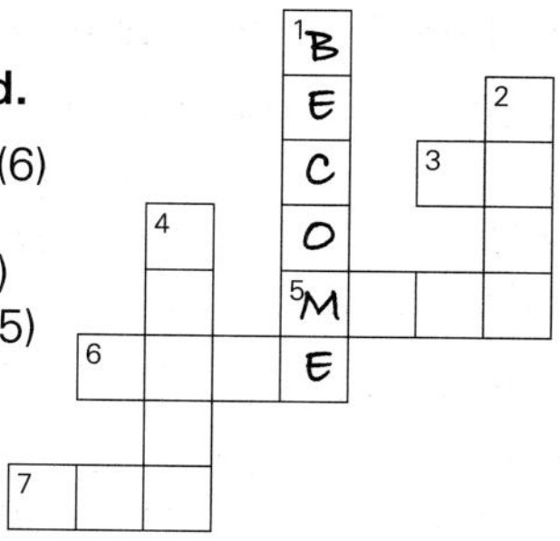

(crossword grid with letters B, E, C, O, M, E)

Grammar: past simple (questions)

2 Complete the questions using the past simple.

Example: When / she / make her first film?
When did she make her first film?

1 When / he / get married?
_____

2 Where / they / go to school?
_____

3 She / go to university?
_____

4 Why / you / move house?
_____

5 You / live in Dublin?
_____

6 When / they / have a baby?
_____

7 Who / she / work for?
_____

3 Complete the questions about David Beckham, a famous English footballer.

Example: *Where did he* live when he was a child?
In Leytonstone, London.

1 _____ start playing for Manchester United?
He started as a trainee in July 1991.
2 _____ play in the 1998 World Cup?
Yes, he did.
3 _____ score his first international goal?
On 26 June 1998, against Colombia.
4 _____ get married?
July 1999.
5 _____ get married to?
Victoria Adams, from the pop group, Spice Girls.
6 _____ have a son or a daughter first?
They had a son, Brooklyn.

21 Quiz show

Vocabulary: numbers

1 Complete the numbers with the correct word.

Example: 3,220: three _thousand_, two hundred _and_ twenty

1 324: three _____ and _____ four
2 8,605: _____ _____, six hundred _____ _____
3 2,179: two _____, one hundred _____ seventy-nine
4 636: six hundred _____ _____-six
5 1,345: one thousand, _____ hundred and _____-_____
6 12,389: twelve thousand, _____ _____ and eighty-nine

Grammar: questions with *How* + adjective

2 Underline the correct adjectives.

Example: How *deep* / *high* is the Empire State Building?

1 How *far* / *long* is Moscow from St Petersburg?
2 How *fast* / *deep* is Concorde?
3 How *long* / *heavy* is the Mississippi River?
4 How *high* / *deep* is the Atlantic Ocean?
5 How *far* / *high* is the Eiffel Tower?
6 How *deep* / *heavy* is a hippo?

3 Match the questions in Exercise 2 with the correct answers.

___ a) 324 m
___ b) 4,200 kg
___ c) 3,780 km
___ d) 2,179 km/h
___ e) 8,605 m
_1_ f) 633 km

4 Write the questions for the answers.

Example:
How high is the Empire State Building?
The Empire State Building? It's about 350 m high.

1 _____?
My office is about 750 m from the station.

2 _____?
I'm about 65 kgs.

3 _____?
My car? Its top speed is about 140 km/h.

4 _____?
The swimming pool is 50 m long. It's Olympic size.

5 _____?
This river? It's not very deep. We can walk across.

22 Sweet and savoury

Vocabulary: countable and uncountable nouns.

1 Are these items of food and drink countable (C) or uncountable (U)?

Example: chocolate _U_

1 cheese ___   5 butter ___
2 wine ___   6 cola ___
3 biscuits ___   7 bread ___
4 sweets ___   8 cakes ___

Grammar: expressions of quantity

2 Look at the pictures. Are the sentences true (T) or false (F)?

Example: There aren't many sweets.   **F**

1 There aren't many biscuits ☐
2 There are a lot of crisps. ☐
3 There's a lot of wine. ☐
4 There isn't much cola. ☐
5 There's a lot of cheese. ☐
6 There isn't much chocolate. ☐
7 There aren't many cakes. ☐
8 There's a lot of bread. ☐

3 Complete the sentences with *much*, *many* or *a lot of*.

Example: How _much_ ketchup is in the bottle?

1 How _____ cheese have you got?
2 I haven't got _____ coffee.
3 Are there _____ biscuits?
4 There's _____ ice cream in the fridge.
5 I don't eat _____ crisps.
6 She always eats _____ sweets.
7 How _____ wine is there in the cupboard?

23 Big plans

Vocabulary: verbs and nouns describing changes in life

1 Match the beginnings of the sentences 1–8 with the ends a)–h).

1 He wants to build a house.
2 I want to retire because
3 Last year I earned
4 She left school
5 I want to give up smoking
6 My parents learned to dance
7 I don't want to change my lifestyle
8 She lost weight …

___ a) £65,000.
___ b) twenty cigarettes a day.
___ c) I'm 65.
___ d) … about 5 kg in the last month.
___ e) because I don't like change.
___ f) when she was 18.
___ g) salsa when they went to Cuba.
_1_ h) because they are expensive to buy.

Grammar: *going to* for future plans

2 Rewrite the sentences with *going to* + verb.

Example: I don't want to buy a new house.
(build) **I'm going to build a new house.**

1 Emily finishes school this year.
(leave) _____

2 We don't want to stop work until we're 70.
(retire) _____

3 Amanda has got a new job – £60,000 a year.
(earn) _____

4 Brian likes smoking. He doesn't want to stop.
(give up) _____

5 My parents want to visit foreign countries.
(go abroad) _____

3 Complete the sentences with the correct form of the verb *be* + *going to*.

A: **_Are_** you **_going to_** go to the USA this year?
B: Yes, I (1) _____. Sally and I (2) _____ go next month.
A: Who (3) _____ you _____ stay with?
B: I (4) _____ stay at my aunt's in Boston.
A: (5) _____ she _____ take you sightseeing?
B: No, she (6) _____. She and my uncle (7) _____ stay at my house in the UK.
A: (8) _____ they _____ go sightseeing?
B: Yes, they (9) _____. They want to visit London.

24 It's on the right

Vocabulary: parts of a public building; American English

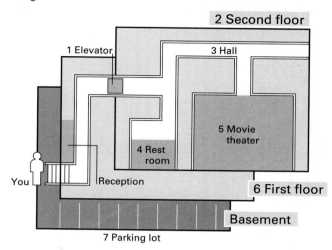

1 Elevator
2 Second floor
3 Hall
4 Rest room
5 Movie theater
6 First floor
Basement
You
Reception
7 Parking lot

1 Look at the map of a building. Write the American place names in British English.

Example: 1 _lift_

2 _____   5 _____
3 _____   6 _____
4 _____   7 _____

Grammar: prepositions of movement

2 Put the sentences in the correct order to make directions from the car park to the toilets.

a) ___ Come out of the lift and go along the corridor.
b) ___ Turn right.
c) ___ OK, go up the stairs from the car park to the ground floor.
d) ___ Turn right and you'll see the lift in front of you.
e) ___ The toilets are in front of you.
f) _1_ Excuse me, where are the toilets, please?
g) ___ Take the lift to the first floor.
h) ___ Turn left, go past reception and go along the corridor.

3 Look at the map and write the directions from the toilets on the first floor to the car park.

A: Excuse me, where is the car park?
B: **OK, Go along the corridor and turn left.**
_____
_____
_____
_____
and you'll see the car park in front of you.

25 Hot and sunny

Vocabulary: weather

1 Find the weather words.

Example: usnny _sunny_

1 yndiw _____

2 gniiainr _____

3 uodlcy _____

4 ngiwons _____

5 oth _____

6 gnieefrz _____

7 dolc _____

8 mawr _____

Grammar: linking words: *because, so, but, although*

2 Make sentences about Sochi, a holiday town near the Black Sea. Match the beginnings of the sentences 1–6 with the ends a)–f).

1 Autumn is cold and wet
2 In winter it is warm because
3 It often snows in the mountains near Sochi so
4 Summer is warm and sunny so
5 Although there are a lot of nightclubs,
6 People swim in summer,

_1_ a) but it is also very beautiful.
___ b) there are a lot of tropical plants.
___ c) although the sea is very cold.
___ d) from October to May you can go skiing.
___ e) they all play the same music.
___ f) Sochi is next to the sea.

3 Complete the sentences with *but, so, because* or *although*.

Example: São Paulo is very hot in summer _so_ a lot of buildings have air conditioning.

1 _____ September in Italy is hot, it can also rain a lot.
2 Many British people go abroad in the winter _____ it's cold and grey in the UK.
3 _____ the south of Spain is hot and dry, the north of Spain is wet and green.
4 It's always hot in Brazil _____ people love going to the beach.
5 Bring a coat _____ don't bring an umbrella _____ it doesn't rain much.

26 A new year

Vocabulary: dates

1 Write the number next to the dates.

Example: first **1**st

1 second	___nd	7 tenth	___th
2 third	___rd	8 twelfth	___th
3 fourth	___th	9 thirteenth	___th
4 seventh	___th	10 fifteenth	___th
5 eighth	___th	11 twentieth	___th
6 ninth	___th	12 thirtieth	___th

2 Match the dates 1–9 with the dates a)–i).

1 1/4/00(UK)
2 15 Feb
3 4/10/02 (US)
4 3 Jul
5 May 13
6 5/8/05 (UK)
7 01-31 (US)
8 16 Dec
9 4/10/02 (UK)

a) 16th of December
b) 1st of April 2000
c) 5th of August 2005
d) Fourth of October 2002
e) 31st of January
f) 10th of April 2002
g) Fifteenth of February
h) Third of July
i) Thirteenth of May

Grammar: time prepositions: *in, on, at*

3 Write the time expressions in the table.

12th December   2005   Wednesday   dinner time
New Year's Day   the evening   October
Saturday   the weekend   21st February
12 o'clock   the morning

In	On	At
	12th December	

4 Underline the correct preposition.

Example: They went on holiday _in_ / on October.

1 They got married *on* / *in* 1999.
2 He started his new job *at* / *on* Monday 8 May.
3 She studied English *in* / *at* the afternoon.
4 He went swimming *in* / *at* the weekend.
5 I got the train *at* / *on* one o'clock.
6 She moved house *in* / *on* November.
7 They had a baby *at* / *on* Wednesday.
8 He finished his university course *in* / *on* 15 June.
9 My family go out together *in* / *at* the evening.
10 I met my husband *on* / *in* July, 1969.

27 Requests

Vocabulary: everyday requests

1 Underline the word in each group which doesn't match the verb.

Example:
to recommend *a sweater / a film / a school*

1 to repeat *speaking / an expression / yourself*
2 to use *a machine / a pen / a cup of coffee*
3 to call *a taxi / a phone / a friend*
4 to pass someone *a car / a book / a glass*
5 to book *a table / a taxi / the receptionist*
6 to pay *for the meal / by credit card / a present*
7 to borrow *your mother / a car / a book*

Function: permission and requests

2 Complete the questions 1–6 and match them with the responses a)–f).

1 Could __I__ borrow a pen?
2 Could _____ recommend a good film?
3 Could _____ use your phone?
4 Could _____ call a taxi for me?
5 Could _____ book a table for six for this evening?
6 Could _____ borrow your red sweater?

___ a) Sorry, I'm afraid we're fully booked.
_1_ b) Sorry, I'm afraid I've only got a pencil.
___ c) Sorry, it's dirty at the moment.
___ d) Yes, of course. Who do you need to call?
___ e) Yes, *The Matrix* is excellent.
___ f) Yes, of course. What time do you want to be collected?

3 Complete the dialogues.

1 A: __Could__ I book two tickets for the show tonight?
 B: Sorry, I'm (1) _____ it is sold out. What about tomorrow?
 A: Yes, that would be fine. Could (2) _____ pay by credit card?
 B: Yes, of (3) _____. What's the number?
 A: 2353 8932.
 B: Could you (4) _____ that again?
 A: Yes, (5) _____. 2353 8932.

2 A: Could (1) _____ recommend a good French restaurant near here?
 B: Yes. Chez Pierre on Fenton Street is very good.
 A: Excellent. (2) _____ you book a table for two at eight this evening for me?
 B: Yes, (3) _____ course.

3 A: Could I use the phone?
 B: I'm (1) _____, someone is using it at the moment.

28 North and south

Vocabulary: adjectives to describe places

1 Match the adjectives with their opposites.

1 hot   a) ugly
2 dry   b) cold
3 clean   c) modern
4 empty   d) mountainous
5 dangerous   e) wet
6 flat   f) safe
7 historic   g) dirty
8 good   h) crowded
9 beautiful   i) bad

Grammar: comparatives

2 Find the mistakes and rewrite the sentences about São Paulo in the south and Recife in the north of Brazil.

Example: It's ~~dryer~~ in São Paulo than Recife.
 It's drier in São Paulo than Recife.

1 São Paulo is more cold than Recife.
 _____

2 Recife is more smaller than São Paulo.
 _____

3 The metro in São Paulo is the more crowded than in Recife.
 _____

4 Accommodation in São Paulo is the most expensive than in Recife.
 _____

5 The population of São Paulo is biger.
 _____

6 I think the lifestyle in Recife is gooder.
 _____

3 Rewrite the sentences using the adjectives.

Example:
Tokyo is more modern than Paris.
(historic) *Paris is more historic than Tokyo.*

1 The north of Italy is more mountainous than the south.
 (flat) _____
2 Poland is colder than Brazil.
 (hot) _____
3 England is wetter than Spain.
 (dry) _____
4 The food in Italy is better than the food in England.
 (bad) _____
5 Small towns are usually safer than big cities.
 (dangerous) _____
6 Japan is smaller than Russia.
 (big) _____

29 The best food in town

Vocabulary: adjectives to describe restaurants

1 Find thirteen more adjectives you can use to describe restaurants.

E	P	R	O	M	A	N	T	I	C
R	O	M	C	C	H	E	A	P	Q
S	P	I	O	L	D	X	E	J	U
T	U	K	M	S	S	P	A	T	I
K	L	O	F	I	C	E	D	O	C
F	A	M	O	U	S	N	A	Q	K
E	R	L	R	A	L	S	E	U	A
P	E	E	T	R	O	I	B	I	G
S	A	S	A	E	W	V	F	E	N
D	R	T	B	R	O	E	Q	T	S
S	M	A	L	L	N	B	U	S	Y
F	R	I	E	N	D	L	Y	P	R

Grammar: superlatives

2 Complete the world records.

Example: __The biggest__ (big) hotel in the world is the MGM Grand in Las Vegas.

1 _____ (long) hotel swimming pool is 541 m at the Hyatt Regency Cerromar Beach Resort in Puerto Rico.
2 _____ (large) department store in the world is Macy's in New York. It is 198,500 m².
3 _____ (expensive) hotel room is the ten-room Bridge Street Suite at the Royal Towers of Atlantis in the Bahamas. It costs $25,000 a night.
4 The Grand Hyatt Shanghai in China is _____ (tall) hotel in the world.
5 The Hotel Everest View in Nepal is _____ (high) altitude hotel in the world at 3,962 m.

3 Use the information in the table to write sentences about the three hotels.

	The Mirador	The Rosary	The Manor
Price (double room per night)	$300	$200	$100
Number of rooms	50	80	75
Comfort guide	*****	****	***
Good food guide	***	**	*****

Example: (cheap) __The Manor is the cheapest.__

1 (expensive) _____
2 (big) _____
3 (small) _____
4 (comfortable) _____
5 (good food) _____
6 (bad food) _____

30 On the phone

Vocabulary: telephones

1 Match the words 1–8 with a)–h) to make telephone expressions.

1 a text
2 directory
3 an area
4 an answering
5 a mobile
6 to take/leave
7 to put
8 to call

a) enquiries
b) code
c) someone on hold
d) message
e) someone back
f) machine
g) a message
h) phone

Function: telephoning

2 Complete the dialogues with these sentences.

has she got your number?
It's 4960008.
she's not in at the moment.
Could you ask her to call me back?
Can I speak to Janine, please?
Hi, this is Angus.
Can I take a message?
Could I leave a message?

1 A: __Hi, this is Angus.__ Is Amy there?
B: Sorry, (1) _____.
A: (2) _____?
B: Yes, sure.
A: Can you ask her to call me?
B: Yes, (3) _____?
A: Yes, she's got it. Thanks.

2 A: Hi, it's Alex. (1) _____?
B: Sorry, she's at work. (2) _____?
A: (3) _____?
B: Has she got your number?
A: No. (4) _____
B: OK. Bye.

3 These words are missing from this telephone conversation. Put them in the correct place.

a   your   in   her   to   can   this   has   me

                        this
A: Hi, ⁄is Pete. Can I speak Mary?
B: Sorry, she's not at the moment. I take message?
A: Yes, please. Could you ask to call back? It's Pete.
B: She got number?
A: No. It's 01632 960 009.
B: OK. Bye.

31 Culture shock

Vocabulary: social etiquette

1 Match the verbs 1–4 with a)–d) to make expressions.

1 give   a) your shoes off
2 wear   b) hands
3 take   c) a suit
4 shake   d) a present

2 Write the expressions from Exercise 1 under the pictures.

1 _____   2 _____

3 _____   4 _____

Grammar: *should* for advice

3 Look at these ideas and write sentences about what you *should/shouldn't* do in the classroom.

• listen to your teacher	• speak your own
• talk on your cellphone	language
• do your homework	• eat food
• work hard	• speak English
• arrive late	• arrive on time

Example: *You should listen to your teacher.*

1 _____
2 _____
3 _____
4 _____
5 _____
6 _____
7 _____
8 _____

32 Party time!

Vocabulary: money verbs

1 Find the money verbs.

Example: yub **buy**

1 ayp _____   4 forfda _____
2 tner _____   5 enspd _____
3 csot _____

2 Complete the sentences using the verbs from Exercise 1.

Example: I really want to **buy** that jacket.

1 It's too expensive. I can't _____ it.
2 I could _____ for it by credit card.
3 How much does it _____?
4 How much money do you _____ on clothes?
5 I want to _____ a car for the weekend.

Function: suggestions

3 Put the words in the correct order.

Example: about going shopping how?
      How about going shopping?

1 I afford really can't it.

_____

2 cinema let's to the go.

_____

3 stay rather at I'd home.

_____

4 rent shall a we video?

_____

5 going on about holiday how?

_____

6 idea that's yes a good.

_____

4 Two friends are planning a birthday surprise for a friend. Complete these dialogue with the words.

going	inviting	let's	about	give	ask
afford	have	rather			

A: How about **going** to a restaurant?
B: I'd (1) _____ go to a bar.
A: (2) _____ buy her a present.
B: Shall we (3) _____ her what she wants?
A: I'd rather (4) _____ her a surprise.
B: How (5) _____ buying her a new camera?
A: Well, we can't really (6) _____ it.
B: Well, OK. But let's (7) _____ a party.
A: How about (8) _____ John?

33 At the movies

Vocabulary: movies

1 Complete the crossword.

	1		2	
3				

⁴S C I E N C E

(crossword grid with numbers 1, 2, 3, 4, 5, 6, 7, 8, 9, 10, 11; 4 across = SCIENCE)

Across

4 (and 3 down) *Star Wars* is a s_____ f_____ film. (7, 7)

5 My favourite a _____ is Brad Pitt. (5)

7 I like a_____ films like *Gladiator*. (6)

9 (and 7 and 8 down) Old films are in b_____ a_____ w_____, not colour. (5, 3, 5)

10 (and 11 across) Computers are needed to make s_____ e_____. (7, 7)

Down

1 The s_____ in *Out of Africa* is beautiful. It was set in Kenya. (7)

2 A c_____ makes me laugh. (6)

3 Go to 4 across.

5 My favourite a_____ is Julia Roberts. (7)

6 *Love Story* is excellent. It is a r_____ film. (8)

7 Go to 9 across.

8 Go to 9 across.

Grammar: *say* and *tell*

2 Underline the correct word in the sentences.

Example: She *said* / *told* she liked shopping.

1 He *said* / *told* me he went to the cinema every weekend.

2 I *said* / *told* that I rarely went to the cinema.

3 Tara *said* / *told* Elizabeth that she loved swimming.

4 Elizabeth *said* / *told* that she hated sport.

5 I *said* / *told* Joanna that I was doing an English course.

6 Joanna *said* / *told* me she didn't want to do a course.

7 She *said* / *told* she was very busy at the moment.

8 Pete *said* / *told* that she worked too hard.

9 He *said* / *told* me his favourite actress was Julia Roberts.

10 They *said* / *told* they didn't like action films.

34 Would you like the menu?

Vocabulary: restaurant words

1 Put these words in the correct category.

knife   bill   spoon   salt   starter   menu   dessert   main course   customer   pepper   fork   waiter

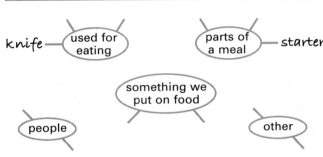

Grammar: *would like/like, would prefer/prefer*

2 Put the words in the correct order. Who would say them? Write C for *customer* or W for *waiter*.

Example: you are order ready to ?   W
Are you ready to order?

1 have bill can please I the? _____

2 would what to you like drink? _____

3 I prefer I'd water please. _____

4 help I you can? _____

5 you a like dessert would? _____

6 like I'd a for please two table. _____

3 Match the questions 1–7 with the correct responses a)–g).

1 Can I help you?

2 Do you prefer red or white wine?

3 What would you like to drink?

4 Would you prefer red or white wine?

5 Are you ready to order your main course?

6 Do you like chicken?

7 Would you like some coffee?

___ a) A glass of wine, please.

___ b) Yes, I do.

_1_ c) Yes, we'd like a table for four.

___ d) I prefer red.

___ e) Yes we are. I'd like the chicken.

___ f) Yes, please. Black, please.

___ g) I'd prefer the red please.

35 Island life

Vocabulary: practical activities

1 Match the verbs 1–7 with the words a)–g).

1 look after
2 use
3 build
4 make
5 teach
6 play
7 grow

a) fruit, vegetables
b) children, English
c) animals, children
d) a digital camera, a laptop
e) a house, a town
f) clothes, a plan
g) a game, an instrument

Grammar: present perfect for experience

2 Complete the verb table.

Infinitive	Past simple	Past participle
to play	*played*	*played*
to use	used	used
to look after	_____	_____
_____	_____	made
to teach	_____	_____
_____	grew	_____
_____	_____	gone/been
to have	_____	_____
_____	did	_____
to build	_____	_____
_____	_____	written

3 Correct the mistakes in the present perfect.

Example: I ~~has~~ never played the piano. ✗ *have*

1 Tyrone has teached English to children.
2 I has looked after my nephews.
3 We have grow some apples.
4 Mary have made a beautiful dress for me.
5 Has Dylan built a new house? Yes, he've.
6 They have never have a dog.

4 Complete the questions in the present perfect.

Example:
A: (use a laptop?) *Have you used a laptop?*
B: Yes, I have. I've got one at home.

1 A: (have pets) _____
  B: No, I haven't. I don't like animals.
2 A: (look after children?) _____
  B: No, he hasn't. He's only 16.
3 A: (go to Madrid?) _____
  B: No, but he went to Barcelona last year.
4 A: (give you a present?) _____
  B: No, she hasn't. I don't expect one.

36 Hard work

Vocabulary: activities at work

1 Underline the word in each group which doesn't match the verb.

Example:
travel   *to work / to the office / <u>to a decision</u>*

1 arrange   *meetings / presentations / clients*
2 give   *a presentation / a talk / long hours*
3 work   *long hours / clients / short hours*
4 drive   *to work / a presentation / to a meeting*
5 meet   *clients / customers / a meeting*
6 make   *decisions / a customer / money*
7 work   *in a team / with clients / a presentation*
8 serve   *a customer / a client / a decision*

Grammar: *have to/don't have to*

2 Complete the sentences about the three jobs with the correct form of *have to/don't have to*. Then match each paragraph (1–3) with a picture.

1 I **have to** work long hours. Sometimes I work for 36 hours without a break. I (1) _____ (not) give presentations but I (2) _____ meet patients. I usually see between 80 and 90 a day. (Picture ___)

2 He (1) _____ travel round the country. He has a car and does about 1,000 km a week. (2) _____ he _____ use the phone? No, his assistant (3) _____ arrange meetings with companies. (Picture ___)

3 What (1) _____ I _____ do? In my job you (2) _____ get up early and serve customers. I have 40 or 50 regulars who always shop with me. My wife and I (3) _____ work as a team because the stall is too busy for one person. (Picture ___)

37 Excuses, Excuses

Vocabulary: parts of the body; illnesses

1 Look at the picture and complete the crossword.

```
1 F  O  O  2 T
          3 T
  4
        5     6
  7
```

2 Find the illnesses/problems.

Example: He's got a (o l c d) _cold._

1 I've got a (g h o u c) _____ .

2 He's got a (a h c h e e d a) _____ .

3 My hand (s t u r h) _____ .

4 She's got a (m p e r t u t a e e r) _____ .

5 My father's got (h a c c k b a e) _____ .

6 I can't speak. I've got a (r s o e t r h a o t)

_____ _____ .

7 He's got a (m o s t a c c h h e a) _____ .

Function: making and accepting apologies

3 Make and accept excuses.

Example:
Sorry / not come to work / headache
I'm sorry, but I can't come to work because
I've got a headache.

1 Afraid / not come cinema / temperature.
   A: _____
   Pity!
   B: _____

2 Sorry / not help / hurt back.
   A: _____
   Worry!
   B: _____

3 Sorry / not talk / sore throat.
   A: _____
   OK!
   B: _____

38 Big issues

Vocabulary: world issues

1 Complete the sentences with these words.

economy space climate population
communication transport politics

Example: Business is going well, so the
economy is strong.

1 _____ in the UK is expensive, especially trains.

2 NASA wants to build a station in _____ .

3 China has the world's biggest _____ with over a billion people.

4 _____ technology like mobile phones and the Internet is faster and cheaper.

5 I don't like _____ . Governments never do what they say.

6 The _____ is getting much hotter and wetter.

Grammar: *will* for predictions

2 Put the words in the correct order.

Example: will hotels space be in there
   There will be hotels in space.

1 not will climate the change.
   _____

2 smaller cities get will.
   _____

3 you be where will year next?
   _____

4 he think doesn't will he be here.
   _____

5 won't use people transport public.
   _____

3 Look at the table and complete the predictions.

In the year 2069	
World population	7 billion
Strongest economy	China
International language	Spanish
Politics	One world government
Most popular transport	Flying cars

Example: In 2069, the world population _will be_
7 billion. (be)

1 China _____ . (have)

2 Many people _____ . (speak)

3 In politics, there _____ . (be)

4 Most people _____ . (drive)

39 Long life

Vocabulary: expressions of time with *for* and *since*

1 Write these time expressions in the table.

March   two years   ages   three o'clock
over a month   Tuesday   17 July   a long time
a couple of months   1980   a week

For	Since
two years	March

Grammar: present perfect: *how long/for/since*

2 Complete the questions in the present perfect.

Example: How long / he / be in his job?
How long has he been in his job?

1 You / have / your jacket / for a long time?
_____

2 How long / she / live there?
_____

3 How long / they / be on holiday?
_____

4 They / know / you / for ages?
_____

5 He / study English / for a long time?
_____

6 How long / we / be married?
_____

3 Complete the sentences in the present perfect.

Example: She**'s been** on the phone for hours. (be)

a) He _____ English for two months. (study)
b) She _____ in the same house in France all her life. (live)
c) We _____ for 25 years, six months, and two days exactly. (be married)
d) They _____ away for two weeks. (be)
e) I _____ this jacket since Christmas. It was a present. (have)
f) No, they _____ me long – only since last week. (not know)

4 Match the answers a)–f) in Exercise 3 to the questions 1–6 in Exercise 2.

Example: 1 *e*

2 __   3 __   4 __   5 __   6 __

40 The perfect job

Vocabulary: work

1 Write these words in the table.

an office   an employee   a salary   a pension
a boss   a colleague   a gym   a crèche

People	Money	Places
		an office

Function: giving opinions, agreeing and disagreeing

2 Put the conversations in the correct order.

1 ___ a) No, I disagree. Weather is important. For example, in hot countries, people sleep in the afternoon.

___ b) No, I don't think so. People work hard in hot and cold places. In my opinion, the weather is not important.

_1_ c) In my opinion, people in cold countries work harder than people in hot countries.

___ d) Yes, but they also start work earlier and finish work later.

2 ___ a) I prefer working from home to working in an office. What do you think?

___ b) That's true, but it's nice to get out of the house.

___ c) Yes, but you have to travel to the office and that takes a long time.

___ d) No, I disagree. I like working in an office and meeting different people.

3 Rewrite the sentences with the words given.

Example: I think that a good boss is very important. (opinion) **In my opinion, a good boss is very important.**

1 Money is the most important thing. Do you agree? (think?) _____ ?

2 A: Employees want good pensions.
   B: Yes, I agree.
   (true) _____

3 Our boss is horrible. What do you think? (agree?) _____ ?

4 I don't think money is everything. (opinion) _____

5 A: A good company should have a good drinks machine.
   B: No, I don't think so. (disagree) _____

Grammar reference

Lesson 1

To be: *am, is, are*

Long form	Short form
I am	I'm
he is	he's
she is	she's
it is	it's
we are	we're
you are	you're
they are	they're

I'm a doctor.
She's interested in music.
They're married.

Lesson 2

Plurals: *What is/are ... ?*

- Add **-s** to most nouns:

a wallet	two wallets
a book	two books

- Add **-es** to nouns ending in **-ch**, **-sh**, **-s** and **-x**:

a watch	two watches
a bus	two buses

- Nouns ending in consonant + **-y**, change **y** to **i** and add **-es**:

a dictionary	two dictionaries
a story	two stories

- Questions
  What is/What's ... ? + singular noun:
  What is your address?
  What's your name?

  What are ... ? + plural noun:
  What are your initials?

Lesson 3

To be (questions and negatives)

Questions	Short answers	
	positive	**negative**
Am I ... ?	Yes, you are.	No, you aren't.
Are you ... ?	Yes, I am.	No, I'm not.
Is he/she/it ... ?	Yes, he/she/it is.	No, he/she/it isn't.
Are we ... ?	Yes, we are.	No, we aren't.
Are they ... ?	Yes, they are.	No, they aren't.

Negatives	
long form	**short form**
I am not	I'm not
you are not	you aren't (you're not)
he/she/it is not	he/she/it isn't (he's/she's/it's not)
we are not	we aren't (we're not)
they are not	they aren't (they're not)

Am I French?	*No, you aren't.*
Is Elton John American?	*No, he isn't.*
Are you happy?	*Yes, we are.*

She isn't English.
We aren't Spanish.

> **Note:** Both short forms for negatives mean exactly the same:
> *we aren't = we're not*

Lesson 4

Possessive adjectives and possessive 's

- Possessive adjectives

Subject pronoun	Possessive adjective
I	my
you	your
he	his
she	her
it	its
we	our
they	their

*What's **your** name?*
***My** name's Rachel.*
***Her** favourite shop is Harrods.*
***Our** favourite book is Dracula.*

- Use possessive **'s** with names:
  This is Sarah's favourite film.
  This is ~~the favourite film of Sarah~~.
  David's eyes are blue.
  ~~The eyes of David~~ are blue.

Lesson 5

Present simple (positive)

- Use the present simple to talk about routines and habits:
  *I **get up** at seven o'clock.*
  *He **watches** television.*
  *They **read** books.*

- Form:
  I/You/We/They   eat
  He/She/It   eats

- Third person singular spelling rules
  – Most verbs add -s in the third person singular:
  He plays football every day.

  – Add -es to **do** and **go**, and verbs ending in -ch, -sh, -s and -x:
  *She do**es**.*
  *He watch**es**.*

  – Verbs ending in consonant + -y, change y to i and add -es:
  *She stud**ies**.*

> Note: have ➜ has
> *I **have** lunch at one o'clock.*
> *She **has** breakfast at seven o'clock.*

Lesson 6

Present simple (questions and negatives)

Questions	Short answers	
	positive	negative
Do I work?	Yes, you do.	No, you don't
Do you work?	Yes, I do.	No, I don't.
Does he/she/it work?	Yes, he/she/it does.	No, he/she/it doesn't.
Do we work?	Yes, we do.	No, we don't.
Do they work?	Yes, they do.	No, they don't.

Negatives	
long form	short form
I do not work.	I don't work.
You do not work.	You don't work.
He/She/It does not work.	He/She/It doesn't work.
We do not work.	We don't work.
They do not work.	They don't work.

*Do you **listen** to music?*   *Yes, I **do**.*
*Does he **have** a bank account?*   *No, he **doesn't**.*

*I **don't meet** people on the Internet.*
*She **doesn't listen** to music on the Internet.*

Lesson 7

A/an, some/any

- Use **a** or **an** when you talk about one thing (singular):
  *I take **a** guide book and **an** umbrella.*

- Use **some** when you talk about more than one thing (plural), but the number is not important:
  *We always take **some** books.*

- Use **any** with questions and plural negatives:
  *Have you got **any** credit cards?*
  *Jack doesn't take **any** books on holiday.*

> Note: Use an with a singular noun which begins with a vowel sound: **an alarm clock** and **an umbrella** (but **a university** and **a uniform**, because these don't begin with a vowel sound).

Lesson 8

Have got

Positive	Negative
I've got a toy.	I haven't got a toy.
You've got a toy.	You haven't got a toy.
He/She/It's got a toy.	He/She/It hasn't got a toy.
We've got a toy.	We haven't got a toy.
They've got a toy.	They haven't got a toy.

Questions	Short answers	
	positive	negative
Have I got a toy?	Yes, you have.	No, you haven't.
Have you got a toy?	Yes, I have.	No, I haven't.
Has he/she/it got a toy?	Yes, he/she/it has.	No, he/she/it hasn't.
Have we got a toy?	Yes, we have.	No, we haven't.
Have they got a toy?	Yes, they have.	No, they haven't.

*I'**ve got** five photo albums. (= I have got)*
*He'**s got** a cat. (= He has got)*
*They'**ve got** some souvenirs. (= They have got)*
*I **haven't got** a collection.*
***Has** he **got** a camera?*
*She **hasn't got** any photos.*
*We **haven't got** any postcards.*
***Have** they **got** any pets?*

Lesson 9

Verbs + -ing

- Use verb + -ing or a noun after these verbs: **like, love, hate** and **don't mind**:
  I like jogging.
  He hates swimming.
  We don't mind aerobics.
  Does he like sports?
  She loves tennis.
  Do you like playing football?
  They don't like golf.

Lesson 10

Asking for information in a shop

- Use **how much** to ask the price of something:
  How much is that jumper?
  How much are the shoes?

- Use **Can I** to ask permission to do something …
  Can I try on the green jacket?

- … and to offer to do something for someone:
  Can I help you?

- Use **this, that, these, those** to indicate things:

	near	far
singular	this	that
plural	these	those

  I like those shoes.
  How much is this shirt?

Lesson 11

There is/are

- Use **there is/there's** + singular noun:
  There is a cinema.
  There's a museum.
  There isn't a theatre.
  Is there a café? No, there isn't.

- Use **there are** + plural nouns:
  There are some cafés.
  There aren't any cinemas.
  Are there any schools? Yes, there are.

Lesson 12

Adverbs of frequency

- To ask about frequency, use **How often … ?**:
  How often do you go to the cinema?
  How often does Mary visit you?

- Use adverbs of frequency (**never, sometimes, usually, often, always**) with the present simple to say how often something happens:
  I often work late.
  She usually goes to a café.
  Peter doesn't often watch TV.
  We sometimes get a takeaway.
  Do they always go out on Saturdays?

> **Note:** Adverbs of frequency go *before* the main verb but *after* the verb **be**:
> *John often runs after work.*
> *It's always noisy.*

Lesson 13

Prepositions of place

- Use prepositions of place (**in, on, next to, opposite, in front of, above, under**) to say where things are:
  There's a computer on the desk.
  Is there a ball under the table?
  The stereo isn't in front of the window.

Lesson 14

Present continuous for now

- Use the present continuous to describe what is happening now:
  Bart's watching his favourite programme.
  I'm not talking to my friends.
  We're enjoying the programme.
  They aren't drinking coffee.
  Are you reading the letter?

- Form: subject + **be** + verb + **-ing**

Positive	Negative
I'm working.	I'm not working.
You're working.	You aren't working.
He's/She's/It's working.	He/She/It isn't working.
We're working.	We aren't working.
They're working.	They aren't working.

Questions	Short answers	
	positive	negative
Am I working?	Yes, you are.	No, you aren't.
Are you working?	Yes, I am.	No, I'm not.
Is he/she/it working?	Yes, he/she/it is.	No, he/she/it isn't.
Are we working?	Yes, we are.	No, we aren't.
Are they working?	Yes, they are.	No, they aren't.

- Spelling rules
  – Add **-ing** to most verbs:
  I'm playing.

  – Verbs ending in consonant + **-e**, take away **e** and add **-ing**:
  The sun's shining.

  – Verbs ending in a consonant + a vowel + a consonant, double the consonant:
  He's sitting down.
  ~~I'm cleanning.~~
  ~~It's rainning.~~

Lesson 15

Making requests

- Use **will** or **can** to ask for things in a café:
  I'll have a tea, please.
  We'll have two chicken sandwiches.
  Can I have a coffee, please?

Lesson 16

Can for ability

- Use **can/can't** + infinitive to talk about your abilities:
  I can speak French. ~~I can to speak French.~~
  He can't drive.
  They can read maps.
  Can she ride a bike? Yes, she can.
  Can we design the website? No, we can't.

- Form:
Positive	subject + **can** + infinitive
Negative	subject + **can't** + infinitive
Question	**Can** + subject + infinitive
Short answers	**Yes** + subject + **can**
	No + subject + **can't**

Note: **Can/Can't** do not change in the third person singular:
He can sing.
~~He cans sing.~~

Lesson 17

Past simple of *be*: *was, were*

Positive	Negative
I was	I wasn't
You were	You weren't
He/She/It was	He/She/It wasn't
We were	We weren't
They were	They weren't

Questions	Short answers	
	positive	negative
Was I …?	Yes, you were.	No, you weren't.
Were you …?	Yes, I was.	No, I wasn't.
Was he/she/it …?	Yes, he/she/it was.	No, he/she/it wasn't.
Were we …?	Yes, we were.	No, we weren't.
Were they …?	Yes, they were.	No, they weren't.

*We **were** young.*
*They **weren't** at work.*
***Were** you happy?*
*There **wasn't** a lot to do.*
*There **weren't** many people to see.*
***Was** there much to do?*

Note: The past simple of **there is/are** is **there was/were**.

Lesson 18

Past simple regular verbs (positive and negative)

- Use the past simple to talk about completed actions in the past, often with a time expression (**yesterday, last Monday** etc.):
  *I **called** New York on Monday.*
  *They **didn't stay**.*
  *She **studied** in London last year.*

- Form:
Positive	subject + past simple
Negative	subject + **didn't** + infinitive

- Spelling rules
  – Add **-ed** to most regular verbs:
  *tal**ked**   visit**ed**   watch**ed***

  – Add **-d** to verbs ending in consonant + **-e**:
  *dance**d**   arrive**d***

  – Verbs ending in consonant + **-y**, change **y** to **i** and add **-ed**:
  *stud**ied**   tr**ied***

Lesson 19

Past simple irregular verbs

- Many verbs are irregular and have irregular past simple positive forms (see the list in the Phrasebook):

I often fall in love.	I *fell* in love last week.
He sometimes buys her flowers.	He *bought* her flowers yesterday.
We meet Sue every Tuesday.	We *met* Sue last Tuesday.

- Form:
Positive	subject + past simple
Negative	subject + **didn't** + infinitive

  > **Note:** The irregular past simple form is only used in positive sentences. The negative and question forms use the infinitive:
  > *Frank **didn't see** Mary at the party.*
  > *Frank didn't saw Mary at the party.*
  > *Did you **give** her a present?*
  > *Did you gave her a present?*

Lesson 20

Past simple (questions)

- Form: **Did** + subject + infinitive?
  *Did you **watch** the film?*
  *Did she **want** to be an actress?*
  *Did they **see** you?*

- As with the present tense, you can use question words (**who**, **when**, **where** etc.) with past simple questions, using the form:
  question word + **did** + subject + infinitive.
  Who did she talk to?
  When did they leave?
  What did you say?

- Short answers:
  Did she talk to you?
  Yes, she did./No, she didn't.
  Did they go on holiday?
  Yes, they did./No, they didn't.

Lesson 21

Questions with *How* + adjective

- Use **how** + adjective to ask questions:
  ***How long** is the River Nile?*
  ***How far** is New York from Boston?*
  ***How heavy** is an elephant?*

Lesson 22

Countable and uncountable nouns

- Some nouns are countable: we can count them and they have a plural form:
  one biscuit, two biscuits

- Other nouns are uncountable – we can't count them and they do not have a plural form:
  butter two butters
  ketchup three ketchups

- Use a singular verb with uncountable nouns:
  *Bread **is** good for you.*
  *Cheese **tastes** nice.*

- Use **many** with countable nouns in questions and negatives:
  *How **many** biscuits are there?*
  *There aren't **many** sweets.*

- Use **much** with uncountable nouns in questions and negatives:
  *How **much** wine is there?*
  *There isn't **much** milk.*

- Use **a lot of** with countable and uncountable nouns in positive sentences:
  *There's **a lot of** cheese.*
  *There are **a lot of** apples.*

Lesson 23

Going to for future plans

- Use **going to** to talk about future plans:
  I'm going to go to Australia.
  He isn't going to go to work.
  She's going to get married.
  Are they going to have a party?
  We're going to learn to cook.

- Form: **be** + **going to** + infinitive

Positive	Negative
I'm going to have a party. He/She/It's going to have a party. We/You/They're going to a party.	I'm not going to have a party. He/She/It isn't going to have a party. We/You/They aren't going to have a party.

Questions	Short answers	
	positive	negative
Am I going to have a party? Is he/she/it going to have a party? Are we/you/they going to have a party?	Yes, I am. Yes, he/she/it is. Yes, you/we/ they are.	No, Im not. No, he/she/it isn't. No, you/we/they aren't.

Lesson 24

Prepositions of movement

- Use prepositions of movement (**up, down, along, past, out of** etc.) to describe where people and things move:
  I went **past** the car park.
  She's going **down** to the basement.

- You can use prepositions of movement to ask for and give directions:
  Come **out of** the lift and **turn left**.
  Do I go **along** Market Street to get there?
  It's **on the right**.

Lesson 25

Linking words: *because, so, but, although*

- Use linking words to join two sentences.

- Use **so** and **because** to explain the reason for an action:
  It was very hot. I went to the beach. (action)
  It was very hot, **so** I went to the beach. (reason for action)
  I went to the beach **because** it was very hot.

- Use **but** and **although** to express opposite ideas:
  I watched the film. I didn't like it.
  I watched the film, **but** I didn't like it.

  Tom was scared of water. He learnt to swim.
  Although he was scared of water, Tom learnt to swim.

  > Note: You can use **although** at the beginning of a sentence but you can't use **but** at the beginning.

Lesson 26

Time prepositions: *in, on, at*

- Use time prepositions to say when things happen:
  I was born **on** 11 June.
  I saw him **at** six o'clock.
  They went to Turkey **in** May.

- Use **in** with: months, years, **in the morning, in the afternoon, in the evening**
  Use **on** with: days, dates, **on Christmas Day, on New Year's Day, on St Valentine's Day**
  Use **at** with: times, **at Christmas, at Easter, at breakfast, at lunch, at dinner**
  I met him **in 1995**.
  His lesson was **in the morning**.
  My course starts **on 1 July**.
  Her birthday is **on Christmas Day**.
  They always talk to each other **at breakfast**.
  I'll see you **at eight o'clock**.

- Don't use a preposition with these words: **yesterday, today, tomorrow, last week/month/year**:
  Bob went to Paris **yesterday**.
  We saw him **last year**.

Lesson 27

Permission and requests

- Use **could** to ask for permission to do something:
  Could I make a cup of coffee?   Yes, sure.
  Could I borrow your car?   Sorry, I'm afraid not.
  Could I open the window?   Yes, of course.

- Use **could** to make requests:
  Could you call a taxi, please? Yes, of course.

- Form: **could** + subject + infinitive
  Could I pay by credit card?
  ~~Could I to borrow that book?~~
  ~~Could you closing the door, please?~~

Grammar reference

Lesson 28

Comparatives

- Use the comparative form of adjectives with **than** to compare two things:
  *It's **bigger than** my town.*
  *The climate is **drier than** in England.*

- It is also possible to compare two things without **than**:
  Which is bigger, France or Spain? France is bigger.

- Form:
  – One syllable ending in a vowel: add -r:
  large ➡ larger

  – One syllable ending in a consonant: add -er:
  cheap ➡ cheaper

  – One syllable ending in consonant + vowel + consonant: double the consonant, add -er:
  fat ➡ fatter

  – Two syllables ending in -y: change **y** to **i**, add -er:
  heavy ➡ heavier

  – Two or more syllables: use **more** + adjective:
  *beautiful ➡ **more** beautiful*

- There are two common irregular comparatives:
  good ➡ better and **bad ➡ worse**:
  *The beer in Belgium is **better** than the beer in the UK.*
  *The pollution in New York is **worse** than in Boston.*

Lesson 29

Superlatives

- Use the definite article and the superlative form of adjectives to compare three or more things:
  *This is **the smallest** restaurant in the world.*
  *It's **the cheapest** meal you can buy.*

- Form:
  – One syllable ending in a vowel: add -st:
  large ➡ largest

  – One syllable ending in a consonant: add -est:
  cheap ➡ cheapest

  – One syllable ending in consonant + vowel + consonant: double the consonant, add -est:
  fat ➡ fattest

  – Two syllables ending in -y: change **y** to **i**, add -est:
  heavy ➡ heaviest

  – Two or more syllables: use **the most** + adjective:
  *beautiful ➡ **the most** beautiful*

- There are two common irregular superlatives:
  good ➡ best and **bad ➡ worst**:
  *That restaurant has **the best** seafood in town.*
  *This restaurant has **the worst** service.*

> **Note:** Use the preposition **in** with the following phrase:
> *the smallest in the world*
> *the smallest ~~of the world~~*

Lesson 30

Telephoning

- Use **This is ...** to tell someone your name on the telephone.
  This is Bernie. ~~I am Bernie~~.

> **Note:** You can use **speaking** in two ways on the phone:
> 1 To add to your introduction:
> *(This is) Bernie speaking.*
> 2 To confirm who you are:
> A: *Could I speak to Bernie, please?*
> B: *Speaking.*

Lesson 31

Should for advice

- Use **should** and **shouldn't** to ask for and give advice. Use **should** to say something is a good idea, and **shouldn't** to say it's a bad idea:
  *Should I bow? Yes, you **should**.*
  *You **shouldn't** take your shoes off.*

- Form:

Positive	subject + **should** + infinitive
Negative	subject + **shouldn't** + infinitive
Question	**Should** + subject + infinitive?
Short answers	**Yes** + subject + **should**.
	No + subject + **shouldn't**.

Lesson 32

Suggestions

- Use **let's**, **shall we?** and **how about?** to make suggestions:
  ***Let's** go out for a meal.*
  ***Shall we** have a party?*
  ***How about** having some champagne?*

- Form:
  Let's + infinitive
  Shall we + infinitive?
  How about + verb + -ing?

Lesson 33

Say and *tell*

- The past tense of **say** is **said**:
  *She **said** that she enjoyed James Bond films.*

- The past tense of **tell** is **told**:
  *He **told me** that he loved this film.*

- Always use an object pronoun (**me, you, him, her, it, us, them**) with **told**:
  *He told **Mary** that Julia Roberts was his favourite actress.*
  *They told **us** that they liked Bond films.*
  ~~*They told that they liked Bond films.*~~

- Never use an object pronoun with **said**:
  She said that she loved Dr No.
  ~~*She said me that she loved Dr No.*~~

- The main verb should be in the same tense as **say/tell**:
  *She **says** that Sean Connery **is** a good actor.*
  *She **said** that she **loved** the special effects.*
  *He **tells** me that Dr No **is** his favourite Bond film.*
  *He **told** me that he **liked** black and white films.*

> **Note:** You can leave out **that**:
> *They told us they liked Bond films.*
> *She said she loved Casablanca.*

Lesson 34

Would like/like, would prefer/prefer

- Use **like** and **prefer** to talk about the things you like in general:
  *I **like** salmon.*
  *He **likes** going to the cinema.*
  *We **prefer** red wine to white.*
  *She **prefers** reading to watching TV.*

- Use **would like** and **would prefer** to say what you want on a particular occasion:
  *I'**d prefer** the pepper sauce, please.*
  ***Would** you **like** a glass of water?*
  *He'**d prefer** to go skiing than sailing.*
  *We'**d like** to watch a really good film.*

> **Notes:** • Using **prefer** indicates a choice between two things.
> • **Prefer** is not usually used in negative sentences.
> • **Would** is usually shortened to '**d** in positive sentences.

like/prefer + noun/verb + -ing	
Positive	
I like He likes	tomatoes. swimming.
I prefer He prefers	vegetables to meat. shopping to working.
Negative	
I don't like He doesn't like	tomatoes. swimming.
Questions	
Do you like Does he like	coffee? trying new food?
Do you prefer Does he prefer	tea to coffee? sitting near the window?

would like/would prefer + noun/to + infinitive	
Positive	
I'd like We'd like	a new car. to leave now.
I'd prefer We'd prefer	a hot drink. to eat out.
Negative	
I wouldn't like We wouldn't like	a new car. to leave now.
Questions	
Would you like Would they like	some olives? to order now?
Would you prefer Would they prefer	some soup? to sit near the window?

Lesson 35

Present perfect for experience

- Use the present perfect to talk about your and other people's experiences. The time that the experience happened is not important:
  I've seen the Taj Mahal. (I've seen = I have seen)
  (= at some time in my life. It doesn't matter when.)

  John has never worked on a farm.
  (= never at any time in his life up to now.)

  > **Note:** You often use the present perfect for experience with **ever** and **never**.
  > *Have you ever met him? No, I've never met him.*

- Form:

Positive	subject + **have** / **has** + past participle
Negative	subject + **haven't** / **hasn't** + past participle
Question	**Have** / **Has** + subject + past participle ?
Short answers	**Yes** + subject + **have** / **has**.
	No + subject + **haven't** / **hasn't**.

- See the list of irregular verbs in the Phrasebook.

  > **Note:** The verb **go** has two past participles: **been** and **gone**. Look at the difference:
  > *Jackie's been to Mexico. ('s been = has been)*
  > (In her life she has visited Mexico.)
  > *Jackie's gone to Mexico. ('s gone = has gone)*
  > (She's in Mexico now.)

Lesson 36

Have to/don't have to

- Use (don't) **have to** to express obligation and necessity:
  *I **have to** work very hard.*
  *He **doesn't have** to meet any customers.*
  *Do you **have to** use a computer at work?*

- Use **have to** to say that something is necessary:
  *I **have to** get up early every day.*
  (My work starts at 7 a.m.)

- Use **don't have to** to say that it isn't necessary:
  *I **don't have to** get up early today – it's Sunday.*
  (I don't go to work on Sunday.)

- Form:

Positive	subject + **have/has to** + infinitive
Negative	subject + **don't/doesn't** + **have to** + infinitive
Question	**Do/Does** + subject + **have to** + infinitive?
Short answers	**Yes** + subject + **do/does**
	No + subject + **don't/doesn't**

  > **Note:** In short answers use the auxiliary verb **do** not **have**.
  > *Do you have to work late?*
  > *Yes, I do.* ~~Yes, I have.~~
  > *No, I don't.* ~~No, I haven't.~~

Lesson 37

Parts of the body: illnesses

- Use **have got** with illnesses and **have hurt** with parts of the body:

I've got a cold.	*He's hurt his arm.*
He's got a sore throat.	*I've hurt my back.*
She's got a temperature.	*She's hurt her arm.*
I've got a cough and a cold.	*I've hurt my leg.*

Making apologies

- Use the present continuous to talk about how you or others are feeling …
  *I'm sorry, but I'm **not feeling** very well.*
  *She's **feeling** a lot better today.*

  … and to make excuses:
  *I can't come to work today because I'm **looking** after my baby brother.*

  > **Note:** Use possessive adjectives with parts of the body:
  > *I've hurt **my** leg.* ~~I've hurt the leg.~~

Lesson 38

Will for predictions

- Use **will** and **won't** to make predictions about the future:
  We'll go on holiday to the moon.
  We won't have satellite television.
  I think we'll use the Internet more.
  I don't think there will be hotels in space.
  Will the population of the world increase in the future?
  Do you think we'll fly private jets instead of driving cars?

- Form:
Positive	subject + **will** ('ll) + infinitive
Negative	subject + **will not** (**won't**) + infinitive
Question	**Will** + subject + infinitive ?
Short answers	**Yes** + subject + **will**
	No + subject + **won't**

> **Note:** When using **think** with **will** /**won't**, be careful of the negatives and short answers:
> *I don't think I'll go.* ~~I think I won't go.~~
> *Do you think we'll survive? Yes, I do.* ~~Yes, I will.~~

Lesson 39

Present perfect: *how long/for/since*

- Use the present perfect to talk about actions or states that started in the past and continue now:
  I've lived here for a long time.
  (I came here a long time ago, and I still live here.)

  We've known each other since 1992.
  (We met in 1992, and we still know each other.)

> **Note:** We often use the present perfect with **how long**, **for** and **since**:
> *How long have you had your dog?*
> *I've had him for two years.*
> *I've had him since last March.*

- Use **for** to talk about the length of time:
  for ages, for five years, for an hour

- Use **since** to say when the action started:
  since last week, since I was a child, since November

Lesson 40

Giving opinions, agreeing and disagreeing

- You can use the expressions **Do you agree?** and **I agree** or **I don't agree** to tell people how you feel and to ask for their opinions:
  I think we should reform our prisons. Do you agree?
  Yes, I agree. ~~Yes, I'm agree.~~
  No, I don't agree. ~~No, I'm not agree.~~

- You can also express your opinions with **I think** and **I don't think**:
  I don't think people take enough exercise, do you?
  ~~I think people don't ...~~

  Do you think we get enough fresh air?
  No, I don't think so.
  ~~No, I don't think it.~~

Recording scripts

1 Meeting people

Exercise 5

Example:
A: Nice to meet you.
B: And you.
1 A: Hello.
 B: Hi.
2 A: How are you?
 B: Fine, thanks.
3 A: Goodbye.
 B: Bye.

Exercise 8

I'm a businessman.
My name's Vanessa.
He's married.
They're doctors.

2 Personal details, please!

Exercise 2

1 battery
2 watch
3 camera
4 mobile phone
5 laptop
6 bag
7 calculator
8 dictionary
9 briefcase
10 wallet
11 pen
12 diary
13 notebook

Exercise 4

S = Salesman   C = Customer

S: Good afternoon, Perfect Presents, Mark speaking, how can I help you?
C: I'd like to order some presents from the catalogue.
S: OK, sir. I just need to ask you a few questions first. What's your surname?
C: Hanson. That's H-A-N-S-O-N.
S: And what are your initials?
C: T P.
S: P P?
C: No, T for Thomas, P for Peter.
S: OK, and what's your address?
C: 8 Kent Road, Bath.
S: And your postcode?
C: SN8 4LD.
S: That's SN8 4LD. And, ur, what are your presents?
C: Number 1, number 2 and number 3.
S: Sorry sir, what are they?
C: No 1 is a battery, number 2 is a watch and number 3 is a camera.
S: OK, a battery, a watch and a camera.
C: Oh no. Two batteries please.
S: OK. Two batteries. Can I take your credit card number, please?
C: Sorry?
S: What's your credit card number?
C: Ummm.... It's ... 0729 9456 3128.
S: And for our information, sir, what's your job?
C: I'm a doctor.
S: And what's your e-mail address?
C: It's tp@hotmail.com.uk

S: OK. Thanks very much.
C: How long …

Exercise 7

job?
your job?
What's your job?

initials?
your initials?
What are your initials?

3 Round the world

Exercise 4

W = Woman   M = Man

W: OK … Leisure and entertainment … oh, OK, jazz isn't French, it's American, and the tango … mmm … the tango is Argentinian. And judo and kendo aren't Chinese. They're Japanese.
M: So … food and drink … the answer to number 1 is b. Paella is Spanish – yes – and the answer to 2 is also b. Sashimi and sushi are Japanese. OK … and the answer to 3 is c. Bigos is Polish.
W: And now famous people. Is top model Gisele Bundchen German? No, she isn't. She's Brazilian. OK … and is J K Rowling British? Yes, she is. And are Elton John and George Michael American?
M: No, they aren't. They're British.

4 Favourite things

Exercise 3

MAR = Margarita   D = David
MIN = Min   J = José

MAR: I love eating out in restaurants. My husband Tim's favourite is the Greek restaurant in our street. The children? Their favourite is Burger King!
D: My wife and I always like to read about the international news. Our favourite newspaper is *The Herald Tribune*.
MIN: I'm from Korea, and I love Harrods, because I can buy everything I want there. Its food hall is excellent. It's expensive, but it's my favourite shop. What's your favourite?
J: The markets in London are excellent! There's so much variety. My favourite is Camden Market, but my sister is different – her favourite market is Borough Market.

5 Celebrations

Exercise 6a

visits
goes
watches

Exercise 6b

1 drinks
2 dances
3 gives
4 eats
5 plays
6 gets

6 The modern world

Exercise 4

P = Presenter   PS = Philip Scholes

P: Today we have Philip Scholes, an expert on communication and technology in the modern world. Philip, do people still contact friends by phone or is it now Internet, Internet, Internet?
PS: Well, ur, 68% of Europeans contact friends by e-mail but 98% also use the phone.
P: And travel? Do Europeans book hotels on the Internet?
PS: 70% of Internet users search for information about hotels. They look, but they don't book online. People use the phone or go to the travel agent's in person.
P: What about school? Do Europeans want to study on the Internet?
PS: Only 35%. 65% want to be in a class with a teacher. They don't want to do a course by computer.
P: And how does your company find its information?
PS: Easy … it doesn't use the Internet. We use the phone.

Exercise 7

Do you
Do you use
Do you use the Internet?

Does he
Does he have a
Does he have a bank account?

7 Travelling

Exercise 8

I take a camera.
An alarm clock is important.
I take some books.
I don't take a personal stereo.
I don't take any guide books.
Do you take any books?

8 The collector

Exercise 5

1 I've got five photo albums.
2 He's got 50 postcards.
3 Have you got a photo collection?
4 Yes, I have.
5 No, I haven't.

9 Top sports

Exercise 5

P = Presenter   CB = Carol Braithwaite

P: … And finally, a new report from the Canadian Fitness Institute, the CFI, shows that Canadians need to get more exercise. Carol Braithewaite, you're a sports psychologist, do we really hate sports?
CB: Well, Canadians don't hate doing sports but we're not very active. The President of the CFI said that 64% of Canadians need to be more active to be healthy. For example, only 21% of us go to a gym and do aerobics.

What the report shows is that men and women like different sports. Men like going jogging and playing golf. Overall, 33% of Canadians go jogging but men also prefer team sports, such as basketball and volleyball. However, only 17% of us play them. Women don't mind playing team games but they love doing aerobics and going swimming and cycling. In total, 57% of Canadians go swimming and 55% go cycling.
P: So what sport do Canadians like the most?
CB: That's an interesting one. Canadians don't like doing sport in general but they love walking. A massive 86% of Canadians say walking is their favourite sport.

10 Shopping

Exercise 4

A = Assistant   C = Customer

A: Can I help you?
C: Yes, have you got this sweater in large?
A: No, sorry, madam. We've only got it in small or medium.
C: OK … mmm … What about these trousers? Have you got these trousers in size 12?
A: No, sorry. Sold out, I'm afraid.
C: Oh! I like that skirt.
A: What colour do you like?
C: Have you got it in red?
A: Sorry, we've only got blue at the moment.
C: What a lovely coat! Have you got it in black?
A: Yes. Here you are, madam.
C: Can I try it on?
A: Yes of course.
C: Thanks.
C: I love it. How much is it?
A: That's £1,000.
C: £1,000? No, thank you!

Exercise 7

How much is it?
Can I try it on?
Can I help you?
Have you got it in blue?

11 Interesting places

Exercise 7

1 There's a small bar.
2 There isn't a market.
3 There aren't any museums.
4 There's a cheap hotel.
5 There are some good cafés.
6 There aren't any interesting shops.

12 The weekend

Exercise 3

P = Presenter   H = Hiroko   M = Marcelo

P: This morning in 'Life Round the World' we look at how people in different countries spend their weekends. We've got some visitors with us in the studio today. Hiroko, you're from Kyoto in Japan, aren't you?
H: Yes.
P: And do you stay in on Friday nights?
H: No, never. I often work late and then I usually go for a drink with my friends. There's a good bar near the office.

P: What do you eat?
H: I never cook on Fridays because I'm usually tired. I go home and get a takeaway from an *Udon* stall.
P: What's *Udon*?
H: Oh, it's a delicious soup with vegetables.
P: Mmm! And onto our next guest … Marcelo, where are you from?
M: I'm from Brazil.
P: And which is your favourite day of the weekend?
M: I love Sundays. I usually go to church in the morning. In the afternoons my wife and I always go to the beach for a walk. We often meet friends there.
P: On the beach?
M: Yes, it's the place where everybody goes. It's always busy on Sundays.
P: Mmm.
M: After that, I sometimes go to the Old Town and have lunch.
P: How often do you go out on Sunday nights?
M: Well, we usually stay in.
P: And Giulia, what do you do at the weekend?

13 Office … or living room?

Exercise 3

C = Christine   RM = Removal man

RM1: Where do you want all this furniture, madam?
C: OK, put the desk over there in front of … in front of the window … no … put it next to the door …
RM2: Next to the door?
C: Hang on, no, put the desk in front of the window. I want to use this room as my new office, you see. Yes, that looks fine. And I'd like the computer and printer on the desk, please.
RM1: On the desk?
C: Yes, next to the telephone … Perfect.
RM2: And where do you want the sofa?
C: In front of the desk. No … next to the door … yes, that's right … next to the door over there.
RM1: Next to the door?
C: Yes … under the calendar. That's perfect.
RM2: And this table?
C: In front of the sofa and put the big plant on the table. Actually no … put them both next to the sofa.
RM2: Next to the sofa? Are you sure, madam?
C: Yes, next to the sofa. And that armchair, put that next to the cupboard … there's a cupboard under the bookcase … hold on, no, put the armchair opposite the desk … and be careful … there's … there's a stereo in the cupboard.

15 Café

Exercise 2

C = Customer   W = Waitress

C1: How much is a chicken sandwich?
W: $5.50.

C2: The ham sandwich. How much is that?
W: $5.95. Tomato is an extra 50 cents.

C3: How much is the cheese sandwich?
W: $5.00.

C4: That cake looks delicious. How much is it?
W: Only $4.85.

C5: How much is a small tea?
W: $1.50.

C6: A large coffee, please. How much is that?
W: $1.95.
C6: And how much is a cola?
W: $1.20.

C7: Those apples look good. How much are they?
W: $1.25.

Exercise 4

C = Customer   W = Waitress

C1: Excuse me, can we have a large coffee, a banana and a chicken and …
C2: Ur …
C1: … yes, a chicken and tomato sandwich.
C2: But, um, …
C1: And I'll have a small tea with lemon and a ham sandwich. No tomato. How much is that, please?
C2: Sorry, I don't work here. There's the waitress.
W: Are you ready to order?
C1: Yes, I'll have a coffee please.
W: Small or large?
C1: Large, please.
W: Anything else?
C1: Yes. A chicken and tomato sandwich and a banana.
W: OK. And …

Exercise 6a

Example:
a Can I have a chicken sandwich? (*polite*)
b Can I have a chicken sandwich? (*rude*)

1 a I'll have a cola. (*polite*)
  b I'll have a cola. (*rude*)

2 a We'll have a coffee. (*rude*)
  b We'll have a coffee. (*polite*)

Exercise 6b

Can I have a chicken sandwich? (*polite*)
I'll have a cola. (*polite*)
We'll have a coffee. (*polite*)

16 Job skills

Exercise 6

I can speak French.
I can't sing.
Can you speak German?
Yes, I can.
No, I can't.

Exercise 7

Example:
I can't read a map.
1 He can't design a website.
2 She can repair a car.
3 Can you type?
4 We can't speak French.

17 Memories

Exercise 3

L = Liam   R = Robbie

L: Your turn, Robbie.
R: OK … holidays.
L: Yes … Where was your best holiday?
R: Well, it wasn't Scotland last year. … I think it was Greece.
L: How old were you?
R: Ur, I was sixteen years old.
L: Why was it good?
R: Well, I was with my family. We were on holiday together for the first time. There wasn't much to do but it was hot and there were beautiful beaches. I loved it!
L: Yeah, it sounds good.
R: OK. Your turn.
L: Yes … um … first love!
R: Right. Who was your first girlfriend?
L: Well, that's easy, it was Emma.
R: What? Your wife Emma?
L: Yes, that's right.
R: Really! How old were you?
L: Oh, we were young. She was about thirteen and I was fourteen.
R: And now you're married! So when's your anniversary?
L: I can't remember.

Exercise 6

A: Was it a good holiday?
B: Yes, it was.

A: How old were you?
B: I was ten.

A: Were the beaches good?
B: Yes, they were.

18 A week in the life of …?

Exercise 6a

visited
called
watched

Exercise 6b

1 studied
2 started
3 finished
4 wanted
5 arrived
6 cleaned
7 talked

19 Love at first sight

Exercise 3

Two years ago Tom met Jane at a party. She was beautiful, intelligent and rich.
Every day he went to her house. He bought her flowers but she wasn't interested. He gave her expensive presents but she still wasn't interested. He even asked her to marry him but she said 'No'.
That day Tom left her house very upset. When Tom came home he cried and cried and didn't think he could love another woman. He thought about Jane all the time.
Six months later he met a woman called Sue.

Tom fell in love immediately. Sue was everything he wanted and she wanted him. He knew it was the real thing and he stopped thinking about Jane.
One day, Tom and Sue went out in their expensive new car. Jane saw them from her house. At that moment, when she saw him with another woman, Jane finally fell in love with Tom … but he didn't love her any more.

20 Life and times

Exercise 6

Example:
When did she become an actress?

1 Who did she work for?
2 Did she go to university?
3 When did she move to New York?
4 Did she get married?
5 When did she get divorced?

21 Quiz show

Exercise 2

Example:
five

1 fifteen
2 twenty-five
3 fifty
4 one hundred
5 two hundred and five
6 two hundred and thirty-five
7 one thousand and fifty
8 one thousand, two hundred
9 seventy-five thousand
10 one hundred and five thousand

Exercise 3

There is one million pounds to be won. Answer question one correctly and you get £25 and for question number two you get £50.
If you get to question number six, you get £1,050. Move on to number eight, and you will win £3,750.
Answer eleven questions correctly, and you win £25,500! And if you are intelligent enough to answer fourteen questions correctly you will win an amazing £500,000!
And if you …

Exercise 6

P = Presenter   C = Contestant

P: So question twelve is for £51,000. If you get the answer right, you'll have £51,000. If you make a mistake you walk away with £25,500. OK. Take your time. How high is Mount Kilimanjaro in Tanzania? Is it … A: 5,895 metres, B: 6,895 metres, C: 3,050 metres or D: 2,050 metres?
C: I think it's A.
P: You said A and now you have £51,000. Well done! OK, the next question is question thirteen, and it's for £100,000. How fast is a cheetah? Is it … A: 102 kilometres per hour, B: 112 kilometres per hour, C: 62 kilometres per hour, D: 142 kilometres per hour?
C: I'm not sure about this one. I know they're fast but I just don't know. I think it's B: 112.
P: Well, you had £51,000. You said B … and the correct answer is B, so you have now got

£100,000. OK … question fourteen. For £500,000. The question is, how long is the River Nile? Is it … A: 6,650 kilometres, B: £8,650 kilometres, C: 1,650 kilometres, D: 4,650 kilometres?
C: I think it's A.
P: Yes! YOU – HAVE – WON – FIVE – HUNDRED – THOUSAND – POUNDS!

22 Sweet and savoury

Exercise 4

P = Presenter   L = Lorraine   M = Melanie
T = Tim

P: Latest statistics suggest that we're becoming a nation which loves sweet food … we went along to our local supermarket to see if it's true … So Lorraine, are you a sweet or savoury person?
L: Sweet, definitely… I can't live without chocolate.
P: So how much chocolate do you eat?
L: A lot. I probably eat some every day.
P: And how many biscuits do you eat?
L: Oh, not many biscuits. I'm a pure chocolate person … oh and chocolate ice cream as well – I eat a lot of that … and chocolate cakes.
P: OK … Melanie, Lorraine eats a lot of chocolate. Have you got a sweet tooth?
M: I don't eat many sweets, really. I'm more a cheese and wine girl.
P: You've got a lot of red wine here, but do you buy much white wine?
M: No, not much.
P: And I see you've got a lot of bread here – how much bread do you eat?
M: A lot. I love bread but I don't have much butter on it … just the bread.
P: And Tim, what about you? Are you a sweet or a savoury person?
T: A bit of both. I eat a lot of biscuits but I always buy a lot of crisps too. I love them … oh and ketchup too, tomato ketchup. I have it on everything, including my crisps.

23 Big plans

Exercise 7

learn English
to learn English
I'm going to learn English.

work
to work
aren't going to work
We aren't going to work.

24 It's on the right

Exercise 3

R = Receptionist   G = Guest

R: Can I help you?
G: Where's the Red Lounge, please?
R: Go along the corridor, past the gift shop. You'll see the lift in front of you. Go up to the second floor. Come out of the lift and turn right. The Red Lounge is on the left.
G: OK, I think I've got that. Thanks.
R: Not at all.

Exercise 6

R = Receptionist   G = Guest

1 G: Excuse me. Where's the restaurant?
   R: There are two, sir. The nearest one is on the first floor. Go <u>up</u> to the first floor, come <u>out</u> <u>of</u> the lift. Turn <u>right</u>, go <u>along</u> the corridor and turn <u>left</u>. You'll see it on the left.
   G: Thank you.

2 R: Can I help you?
   G: Is there a gym here?
   R: Yes madam, it's on the third floor. Come out of the lift and turn <u>left</u>. Go <u>past</u> the cinema and then turn <u>right</u>. The gym is on the <u>right</u>.

3 G: Where's the parking lot?
   R: Sorry, sir. Could you say that again?
   G: The parking lot.
   R: Oh, the car park. Yes, go <u>past</u> the gift shop and take the lift. Go <u>down</u> to the basement. Come <u>out</u> <u>of</u> the lift and you'll see it <u>in</u> <u>front</u> <u>of</u> you.

26 A new year

Exercise 3

1 The second of August, oh two.
2 January the twenty-third, two thousand and one.
3 The fourteenth of March.
4 July the fourth, oh one.
5 The third of November.
6 The twelfth of April, two thousand and two.
7 The twenty-fifth of February, oh two.
8 The sixteenth of January.

Exercise 4

P = Presenter   D = Dave
J = Jennifer   G = George

P: Time to 'Think About The Past'. Remember 1999, the last year of last century? We want to know where you were and what you did in 1999. So, on line one we have Dave from Oxford. What can you remember, Dave?
D: Well, not very much. No seriously, I went to Sydney to see my family. On 31 December, we went to see the celebrations in the centre. It was like a big party and at twelve o'clock they had these incredible fireworks and music. I'll never forget that!
P: Yes, that was good, I remember watching it on TV. Thanks very much for your call, Dave. And on line two we have Jennifer. Where were you in 1999, Jennifer?
J: I was in England. I remember trying to watch the eclipse in August. I bought the special glasses and I didn't go to work. It was on a Wednesday, at about eleven o'clock in the morning, and we all looked at the sky but we couldn't see anything because it was cloudy. It was very disappointing.
P: Yes, I remember that too. It was on 11 August, wasn't it? Well, maybe next time, Jennifer! Thanks for your call. And George on line three?
G: Well, I remember making a lot of money. I'm a computer consultant. In November and December I spent most of the time in an office repairing computers so they worked for the year 2000. Everyone was very worried about their computers around the millennium and then nothing happened!

P: Yes, I was one of those worried people. Thanks for calling George … and coming up next on SFM, the latest news and weather …

27 Requests

Exercise 5

1 A: Could you pass the coffee, please?
   B: Yes, of course.

2 A: Could I borrow your pen, please?
   B: Sorry, I'm using it.

3 A: Could you recommend a good restaurant?
   B: Yes, the Gold Star's not bad.
   A: OK, thanks.

4 A: Could I pay by cheque, please?
   B: Sorry, I'm afraid we don't accept cheques.

Exercise 8

1 A: Could you pass the wine, please?
   B: Sure. Red or white?

2 A: Could I borrow your car, please?
   B: Sorry, I'm going to the airport so I need it.

3 A: Could I pay by credit card?
   B: Yes of course. Visa or Amex?

4 A: Could you say that again, please?
   B: Yes, I said my name is Sara.

5 A: Could you recommend a good restaurant?
   B: Sorry, I'm new around here.

6 A: Could I use your mobile phone?
   B: Yes, sure. Press the green button to call.

7 A: Could I have a coffee, please?
   B: Yes, of course. Milk and sugar?

8 A: Could you tell me the way to the Tower Hotel?
   B: Yes. It's down this street on the left.

28 North and south

Exercise 4

R = Reporter   S = Speaker

R: Once again it's 'New Zealand's 'Favourite Place' competition and I'm here in Wellington, the capital, to ask people which place they want to win. Tell me … which is your favourite place?
S1: Auckland. There are about one million people there so it's bigger and more modern than the other cities and the shopping is great. And here in the North Island you're close to interesting places like Rotorua where you can learn about traditional Maori culture. People in the South Island say we're not very friendly but that's true for all big cities.
R: … and for you, North Island or South Island?
S2: I want the province of Marlborough to win. The climate is drier in the South Island so it's a good place to grow wine, especially white wine. It's also close to the Southern Alps. It's more mountainous than the North Island – you can go walking in the Mount Cook National Park and not see another person for days.
R: Tell us about your choice.
S3: I want Queenstown to win. It's wetter than other places in New Zealand but more exciting because you can do any adventure

sport you want and the shops are open seven days a week. This town in the South Island is where they invented bungee jumping in the 1980s. It can get very crowded with people coming from all over the world but there's always a good atmosphere.

Exercise 7

bigger
bigger than
It's bigger than here.

more modern
more modern than
It's more modern than here.

29 The best food in town

Exercise 2

<u>fa</u>mous
<u>bu</u>sy
<u>qui</u>et
<u>friend</u>ly

<u>com</u>fortable
<u>pop</u>ular

<u>ro</u>mantic
ex<u>pen</u>sive

30 On the phone

Exercise 5

W = Woman   M = Man

W: Hello.
M: Hi, this is Tom. Can I speak to Sue?
W: Sorry, she isn't here at the moment. Can I take a message?
M: Yes, please. Could you ask her to call me back? It's Tom.
W: Call Tom … Has she got your number?
M: It's 01632 895506.
W: So that's 01632 895506.
M: Thanks very much. Bye.

31 Culture shock

Exercise 3

W = Woman   M = Man

W1: OK, that's the end of my talk. So, any questions?
M1: Yes, I want to ask about meetings. When should we arrive?
W1: Good question. For business appointments, you should definitely arrive on time or possibly five minutes early.
W2: Should we bow when we meet people?
W1: Well, greeting people in the UK or the US is a little different. It's not important if you're young or old … you shake hands with everyone. Also, you shouldn't use first names. Wait until they call you by your first name and then you can do the same.
M2: What about invitations? What should we do when we visit someone's house?
W1: I'm glad you asked that question. When you go to someone's house for dinner, you should take a bottle of wine or a small present. But there's one big difference from Japan … you shouldn't take your shoes off. I did that on my first visit and I was the only person in the room with no shoes.

W3: So what should we wear?
W1: For formal business meetings, you should wear a suit. For social occasions, you can ask your host. They're usually very friendly … I know, I married one!

Exercise 5

Example:
<u>Should</u> I wear a <u>suit</u>?

1 <u>Should</u> I take a <u>present</u>?
2 <u>Yes</u>, you <u>should</u>.
3 <u>Should</u> you use <u>first</u> names?
4 <u>No</u>, you <u>shouldn't</u>.

32 Party time!

Exercise 3

PO = Party organiser   C = Client

PO: Hello, nice to see you again. So, you're having another end of year party. Do you want to do it the same as last year or do you want to make some changes? How about having a fancy dress party? We've got some good offers on at the moment.
C: No, I'd rather have a smaller party this year … we can't really afford a big one at the moment. Um … can we look at how much we spent last year and then we can decide together what to do?
PO: OK. First things first, where do you want to have it? Shall we rent the room at the Sheraton again?
C: No, let's have it at the office this time. We don't need to pay for somewhere when we've got the Levine Suite, you know … where we have the conferences.
PO: Yes, that's fine. So how about the food and drink?
C: Yes, the food was great last year, but let's have the wine and not the champagne this time. Ur, we can't really afford the champagne.
PO: And how about the music? This year we have a special karaoke offer. Are you interested?
C: Yeah, let's do that. Um … how much does it cost?
PO: I'm sure we can give you a good price. What do you want to do about …

Exercise 6a

A: How about having a party?
B: Yes, that's a good idea.
A: Shall we have it at the office?
B: Let's have it in a nightclub.

34 Would you like the menu?

Exercise 4

W = Waiter   C = Customer

W: Good evening sir, good evening madam. Would you like a table for two?
C1: Yes, please.
W: And what would you like to drink?
C1: Can I see the wine list please?
W: Yes, sir. Do you prefer red or white wine?
C1: I prefer red.
W: Then I can recommend the house red, sir.
C1: Fine.
W: Are you ready to order now?
C2: Yes, but what's the Salmon Ritz?

W: That's very good … it's salmon in a pepper sauce with tomatoes and olives.
C1: Mmm! And the Salmon Savoy, what's that?
W: That's delicious. Do you like olives?
C1: Yes, I do.
W: Well, it's salmon in a green olive sauce with tomatoes and pepper.
C2: And could you tell me about the Salmon Plaza?
W: Ooooh, that's our speciality – salmon in a tomato sauce with black olives, topped with pepper. Lovely!
C1: OK. I really like olives so I'd like the Salmon Savoy.
W: And madam, what would you like?
C2: I'd like the Salmon Ritz.
W: And would you prefer mixed salad or mixed vegetables?
C1: What are the vegetables?
W: Tomatoes and olives.
C1: I'd prefer the mixed salad.
W: Any starters? We've got a lovely soup with …
C1 + C2: … tomatoes , olives and pepper?

Exercise 7

1 I'd like some cheese.
2 Do you like black coffee?
3 I'd prefer red wine.

36 Hard work

Exercise 7

have to
have to serve customers
I have to serve customers.

have to
Does he have to
Does he have to meet clients?

37 Excuses, excuses

Exercise 6

T = Tony   R = Roger

Monday
T: Can I speak to Roger please?
R: Speaking.
T: Roger, I'm really sorry but I'm not feeling very well. I've got a bad cough and I can't come to work today.
R: OK. Don't worry. Let me know if you can't come in tomorrow.
T: OK. Bye.

Tuesday
T: Hello, Roger, it's Tony. I'm afraid I can't come to work today. I've got a cold and I've got a temperature too. I'm just going to stay in bed, I think.
R: That's OK. Hope you get better soon.

Thursday
T: Roger, Tony here. Listen, I'm sorry but I 've got a stomachache.
R: What a pity!
T: Yeah, I think it was something I ate. It's probably just a 24-hour thing.
R: OK. Um, give me a ring tomorrow and let me know how you are.

Friday
T: Roger …
R: Tony … let me guess, you've hurt your back and you can't move.

T: How did you know?
R: Relax, Tony … stay in bed … take as long as you want. In fact, don't come back on Monday. You've lost your job. A client saw you yesterday on your mobile … at a hotel … on holiday.

Exercise 8

sorry   cold
I'm sorry, but I've got a cold.

                    pity
What a pity!

38 The future

Exercise 3b

Example:
tech<u>no</u>logy

<u>po</u>litics
<u>trans</u>port
<u>space</u>
<u>cli</u>mate
<u>po</u>pulation
e<u>co</u>nomy
communi<u>ca</u>tion

Exercise 7

1 I'll
2 I won't
3 will
4 they'll

40 The perfect job

Exercise 4

P = Presenter   PS = Psychologist
M = Manager

P: With us today we have Nina Hooper, a professor of psychology …
PS: Hello.
P: … and Matt King, a manager of an advertising company …
M: Hello.
P: Matt King, as a manager, what do you think is the most important thing for the perfect job? Do you agree that it's still money?
M: No, I don't think so. A lot of bosses are making offices like homes. They have sofas, cafés, crèches … and I think people work hard when they feel relaxed.
PS: Yes, but some companies are doing too much. For example, I think a dating agency in the office is crazy! I don't think office relationships work.
M: That's true.
PS: In my opinion, employees still want a high salary and a good pension when they retire. That's more important than games rooms and bars at work. Employees do like a good working environment, of course, but at the end of the day, they want the money.
M: No, I disagree. The employees I talk to all say the most important things are friendly colleagues and a good boss.
PS: Let's agree to disagree on that!

Practice section answer key

1 Meeting people

1 2 c 3 a 4 b

2

```
C V G U O P S C U I P A
E R M U Q Z U O D R O L
F M U S I C O A D N L M
S A X A U I Q W A F A O
G R H J X S T U D E N T
I R U V B M E A O N D P
S I N G L E Y R C Y T F
Y E R P Q E J L T R U I
F D S C B N S P O R T L
P A B R A Z I L R Y O M
S D C V R T H O P S Z S
B U S I N E S S M A N X
```

3 1 'm 2 's 3 are 4 're 5 'm 6 'm
7 're 8 'm 9 's

2 Personal details, please!

1 1 pen 2 bag 3 watch 4 pen
5 camera 6 camera

2 -s: cameras; notebooks; mobile phones;
laptops; bags; briefcases; calculators; pens;
wallets
-ies: batteries; diaries; dictionaries
-es: watches

3 1 What is your name/surname?
2 What are your initials?
3 What are your first names?
4 What's your postcode?
5 What's your address?
6 What's your job?
7 MPB@alloallo.com.uk

3 Round the world

1 1 Irish 2 France 3 American
4 Argentinian 5 Russian 6 Japanese

2 1 Carmen and her husband are doctors.
2 Mehmet isn't a businessman.
3 Carmen's (is) married.
4 Mehmet and Carmen aren't interested in
books.
5 Carmen and Mehmet aren't French.

3 1 am 2 are 3 'm 4 are 5 Are 6 am
7 's 8 's 9 'm

4 Favourite things

1 Across: 1 museum 5 book 6 sport
8 programme 9 market
Down: 2 shop 3 magazine 4 newspaper
5 bar 7 film

2 1 's 2 my; your 3 Their 4 our; their
5 's; Her 6 's; His; Its

5 Celebrations

1 1 an instrument 2 water 3 a present
4 to music 5 for a walk 6 to bed
7 to bed 8 ice cream

2 1 goes 2 play 3 go 4 gets 5 dance
6 visit 7 eats 8 drinks

3 1 cook 2 have/eat 3 watches 4 play
5 go

6 The modern world

1 1 buy 2 meet 3 speak to 4 book
5 do 6 have 7 listen to

2 1 I don't buy new books on the Internet.
2 Nicole doesn't speak to her friends by
e-mail.
3 She doesn't meet new friends in Internet
chat rooms.
4 They don't listen to music in cafés.
5 Ryan doesn't have a bank account on the
phone.
6 He doesn't book holidays in a travel
agent's.
7 I don't want to do an English course on the
Internet.
8 Jim doesn't do a computing course with a
private teacher.

3 1 Do they book hotels on the Internet?
2 Does he do a German course with a private
teacher?
3 When do you speak to your friends?
4 Does Marianna meet new friends at
school?
5 Where do you meet people?
6 What do they buy on the Internet?
7 Does Trevor buy music in a shop or on the
Internet?
8 Do Sarah and Nicky study French?

7 Travelling

1 1 car 2 taxi 3 bicycle 4 tram
5 subway 6 boat 7 plane 8 bus

2 2 an umbrella 3 a camera
4 some swimming trunks
5 some books 6 an alarm clock
7 some travellers' cheques 8 a film

3 1 any 2 any 3 an 4 a 5 any
6 some

8 The collectors

1 1 a 2 b 3 b 4 a

2 1 He hasn't got a book. He's got a
newspaper.
2 She's got a mug. She hasn't got a plate.
3 They haven't got a poster. They've got a
photo album.

3 1 Has Joanne got a poster of Brad Pitt?
2 Have you got a favourite mug?
3 Have Marie and Paul got any collections?
4 Have they got a car?
5 Has he got a big house?
6 Has she got any ornaments?

9 Top sports

1

```
S W I M M I N G W V L
A K S K I I N G A O C
B A S K E T B A L L Y
I R N A E E L I K L C
L A G T A N A N I E L
L T I G O N O G N Y I
A E R O B I C S G B N
I O L L S S D O C A G
N A E F O O T B A L L
G J O G G I N G J L W
```

2 Use a ball: tennis; basketball; football; golf;
volleyball
No ball: jogging; swimming; skiing; aerobics;
karate; walking; cycling

3 1 Tara likes doing aerobics.
2 Tara doesn't mind going swimming.
3 Tara doesn't like going jogging.
4 Tara hates playing golf.
5 Steven loves doing karate.
6 Steven likes playing volleyball.
7 Steven doesn't mind playing football.
8 Steven doesn't like playing basketball.
9 Steven hates going cycling.

10 Shopping

1 1 trousers 2 skirt 3 shorts 4 sweater
5 jacket 6 suit 7 trainers 8 shoes
9 boots 10 coat

2 2 Have you got it in green?
3 What size are you?
4 Can I try it on?
5 How much is it?

3 2 d 3 b 4 a 5 c

11 Interesting places

1 1 The clothes in Guccio are very expensive. A
shirt costs over £50.
2 People in cities like London are very
unfriendly and never talk to you.
3 I think English food is good.
4 My house is very busy at the weekends.
There are lots of people.
5 There's a really interesting film on at the
cinema. Do you want to go?
6 That watch looks expensive. How much is
it?
7 His English is very bad so talk slowly.

2 1 Is there a museum?
2 There's a big restaurant.
3 There's a good bar.
4 There isn't a cinema.
5 Are there any hotels?
6 There are some markets.

12 The weekend

1 2 h 3 d 4 b 5 f 6 a 7 g 8 e

2 1 How often do you stay in?
2 Do you sometimes get a takeaway?
3 No, I never get a takeaway.
4 I am always late.
5 Is it often busy?
6 They usually meet friends on Sundays.

3 1 I usually meet my friends at about nine
o'clock.
2 I never go to the gym.
3 He often works late.
4 I am always happy to get a takeaway.
5 They are often quiet after school.
6 My family usually stays in once a week.

Practice section answer key

13 Office ... or living room?

1
```
S B O U G X Y D L O O X
M B K S T E R E O V M N
M O Q D E S K W F O C B
S G E P L A N T V F O B
O C O C E A X K C T Q C
F P C U P B O A R D J X
A R M C H A I R Q U Q Z
W Y B O O K C A S E L A
N P R I N T E R Z F A E
V C A L E N D A R R M S
Q D B I N Z Y M X P P Q
M W Q U C Y O C W J H J
```

2 1 under 2 in front of 3 in 4 next to
5 on 6 above 7 opposite 8 on
9 next to

14 Family

1 Men: brother; father; grandfather; husband;
son; uncle
Women: aunt; daughter; wife; sister; mother;
grandmother
Both: children; parents

2 dance – dancing; watch – watching;
talk – talking; get – getting; study – studying;
use – using; give – giving; sit – sitting;
have – having; go – going; swim – swimming;
do – doing; play – playing; smoke – smoking

3 1 's drinking 2 are sitting
3 's wearing; 's talking 4 are standing
5 's taking

15 In a café

1 Hot drinks – cola; Cold drinks – chicken;
Fruit – cheese; Cake – tomato

2 1 I'll have a chicken sandwich.
2 I'll take your order now.
3 Can we have two large coffees, please?
4 Can I have an apple, please?
5 The children will have cola.
6 Can I have a cheese sandwich with extra
tomato?

3 1 I'll have; Anything; Can I
2 Can I have; Here; How much
3 'll have; can I have

16 Job skills

1 to type – a letter; to sing – a song;
to manage – people; to repair – a car;
to design – a car; to drive – a car

2 1 can't drive 2 can read 3 can manage
4 can't design 5 can't type; can
6 can't speak 7 can't repair

3 1 Can you drive 2 can 3 Can he play
4 Can they design 5 he can't

17 Memories

1 1 Who 2 Where 3 How old
4 How many 5 How much 6 What

2 2 c 3 b 4 f 5 a 6 e

3 1 1 was 2 was 3 were
2 1 was 2 was 3 were 4 was
3 1 were 2 was 3 was 4 were

4 1 My school was in Scotland.
2 My friends weren't on holiday.
3 They were at work.
4 I was good at cycling.
5 What were you interested in?

18 A week in the life of ...

1 2 c 3 d 4 f 5 a 6 e 7 b

2 1 We didn't want to go to university.
2 Lessons didn't start at 8:30 in the morning.
3 My friends didn't study French.
4 Tony didn't watch French films.
5 I didn't play football every Wednesday.

3 1 started 2 stayed 3 cooked
4 didn't study 5 talked 6 watched
7 didn't play 8 didn't have 9 didn't want
10 visited 11 didn't dance 12 called

19 Love at first sight

1 to go – went; to have – had;
to come – came; to say – said;
to think – thought; to buy – bought;
to do – did; to leave – left; to see – saw;
to fall – fell; to meet – met; to give – gave

2 2 a 3 f 4 b 5 h 6 c 7 e 8 g

3 1 She *went* to work.
2 She *drank* a cup of coffee.
3 She *didn't eat* a sandwich at work.
4 She *met* Ann at lunch time.
5 She *didn't buy* any flowers.
6 In the evening they *didn't go* to a
restaurant.
7 She *gave* Eve a present.

20 Life and times

1 Across: 3 do 5 make 6 have 7 get
Down: 1 become 2 move 4 start

2 1 When did he get married?
2 Where did they go to school?
3 Did she go to university?
4 Why did you move house?
5 Did you live in Dublin?
6 When did they have a baby?
7 Who did she work for?

3 1 When did he 2 Did he 3 When did he
4 When did he 5 Who did he 6 Did they

21 Quiz show

1 1 three *hundred* and *twenty*-four
2 *eight thousand*, six hundred *and five*
3 two *thousand*, one hundred *and*
seventy-nine
4 six hundred *and thirty*-six
5 one thousand, *three* hundred and *forty-five*
6 twelve thousand, *three hundred* and
eighty-nine

2 1 far 2 fast 3 long 4 deep 5 high
6 heavy

3 2 d 3 c 4 e 5 a 6 b

4 1 How far is your office from the station?
2 How heavy are you?
3 How fast is your car?
4 How long is the swimming pool?
5 How deep is this river?

22 Sweet and savoury

1 1 U 2 U 3 C 4 C 5 U 6 U 7 U
8 C

2 1 F 2 T 3 F 4 T 5 F 6 F 7 F
8 F

3 1 much 2 much 3 many 4 a lot of
5 many 6 a lot of 7 much

23 Big plans

1 2 c 3 a 4 f 5 b 6 g 7 e 8 d

2 1 Emily's going to leave school this year.
2 We aren't going to retire until we're 70.
3 Amanda's going to earn £60,000.
4 Brian isn't going to give up smoking.
5 My parents aren't going to go abroad.

3 1 am 2 are going to 3 are; going to
4 'm going to 5 Is; going to 6 isn't
7 are going to 8 Are; going to 9 are

24 It's on the right

1 2 first floor 3 corridor 4 toilets
5 cinema 6 ground floor 7 car park

2 2 c 3 h 4 d 5 g 6 a 7 b 8 e

3 **Suggestions**
OK, go along the corridor and turn left. Take
the lift to the ground floor.
Come out of the lift and turn left. Go along
the corridor and go past reception. Turn right
and go down the stairs and you'll see the car
park in front of you.

25 Hot and sunny

1 1 windy 2 raining 3 cloudy 4 snowing
5 hot 6 freezing 7 cold 8 warm

2 2 f 3 d 4 b 5 e 6 c

3 1 Although 2 because 3 Although 4 so
5 but; because

26 A new year

1 1 2nd 2 3rd 3 4th 4 7th 5 8th
6 9th 7 10th 8 12th 9 13th 10 15th
11 20th 12 30th

2 2 g 3 f 4 h 5 i 6 c 7 e 8 a 9 d

3 In: 2005; the evening; October; the morning
On: 12th December; Wednesday; New Year's
Day; Saturday; 21st February
At: dinner time; the weekend; 12 o'clock

4 1 in 2 on 3 in 4 at 5 at 6 in 7 on
8 on 9 in 10 in

27 Requests

1 1 speaking 2 a cup of coffee 3 a phone
4 a car 5 the receptionist 6 a present
7 your mother

2 2 you (e) 3 I (d) 4 you (f) 5 I (a)
6 I (c)

3 1 1 afraid 2 I 3 course 4 say 5 sure
2 1 you 2 Could 3 of
3 1 sorry

28 North and south

1 2 e 3 g 4 h 5 f 6 d 7 c 8 i 9 a

2 1 São Paulo is colder than Recife.
2 Recife is smaller than São Paulo.
3 The metro in São Paulo is more crowded
than in Recife.
4 Accommodation in São Paulo is more
expensive than in Recife.

5 The population of São Paulo is bigger.
6 I think the lifestyle in Recife is better.

3 1 The south of Italy is flatter than the north.
2 Brazil is hotter than Poland.
3 Spain is drier than England.
4 The food in England is worse than the food in Italy.
5 Big cities are usually more dangerous than small towns.
6 Russia is bigger than Japan.

29 The best food in town

1

E	P	R	O	M	A	N	T	I	C
R	O	M	C	C	H	E	A	P	Q
S	P	I	O	L	D	X	E	J	U
T	U	K	M	S	S	P	A	T	I
K	L	O	F	I	C	E	D	O	C
F	A	M	O	U	S	N	A	Q	K
E	R	L	R	A	L	S	E	U	A
P	E	E	T	R	O	I	B	I	G
S	A	S	A	E	W	V	F	E	N
D	R	T	B	R	O	E	Q	T	S
S	M	A	L	L	D	N	B	U	S	Y
F	R	I	E	N	D	L	Y	P	R

2 1 The longest   2 The largest
3 The most expensive   4 the tallest
5 the highest

3 1 The Mirador is the most expensive.
2 The Rosary is the biggest.
3 The Mirador is the smallest.
4 The Mirador is the most comfortable.
5 The Manor has the best food.
6 The Rosary has the worst food.

30 On the phone

1 2 a   3 b   4 f   5 h   6 g   7 c   8 e

2 1 1 she's not in at the moment.
2 Could I leave a message?
3 has she got your number?
2 1 Can I speak to Janine, please?
2 Can I take a message?
3 Could you ask her to call me back?
4 It's 4960008.

3 A: Hi, *this* is Pete. Can I speak *to* Mary?
B: Sorry, she's not *in* at the moment. *Can* I take *a* message?
A: Yes, please. Could you ask *her* to call *me* back? It's Pete.
B: *Has* she got *your* number?
A: No. It's 01632 960009.
B: OK. Bye.

31 Culture shock

1 2 c   3 a   4 b

2 1 shake hands   2 give a present
3 wear a suit   4 take your shoes off

3 1 You shouldn't talk on your cellphone.
2 You should do your homework.
3 You should work hard.
4 You shouldn't arrive late.
5 You shouldn't speak your own language.
6 You shouldn't eat food.
7 You should speak English.
8 You should arrive on time.

32 Party time!

1 1 pay   2 rent   3 cost   4 afford   5 spend

2 1 afford   2 pay   3 cost   4 spend   5 rent

3 1 I can't really afford it.
2 Let's go to the cinema.
3 I'd rather stay at home.
4 Shall we rent a video?
5 How about going on holiday?
6 Yes, that's a good idea.

4 1 rather   2 Let's   3 ask   4 give   5 about
6 afford   7 have   8 inviting

33 At the movies

1 Across: 4 science   5 actor   7 action
9 black   10 special   11 effects
Down: 1 scenery   2 comedy   3 fiction
5 actress   6 romantic   7 and   8 white

2 1 told   2 said   3 told   4 said   5 told
6 told   7 said   8 said   9 told   10 said

34 Would you like the menu?

1 Used for eating: knife; spoon; fork
Parts of a meal: starter; dessert; main course
People: customer; waiter
Something we put on food: salt; pepper
Other: bill; menu

2 1 Can I have the bill, please? (C)
2 What would you like to drink? (W)
3 I'd prefer water, please. (C)
4 Can I help you? (W)
5 Would you like a dessert? (W)
6 I'd like a table for two, please. (C)

3 2 d   3 a   4 g   5 e   6 b   7 f

35 Island life

1 2 d   3 e   4 f   5 b   6 g   7 a

2 to play – played – played;
to use – used – used;
to look after – looked after – looked after;
to make – made – made;
to teach – taught – taught;
to grow – grew – grown;
to go – went – gone/been;
to have – had – had;
to do – did – done;
to build – built – built;
to write – wrote – written

3 1 Tyrone has *taught* English to children.
2 I *have* looked after my nephews.
3 We have *grown* some apples.
4 Mary *has* made a beautiful dress for me.
5 Has Dylan built a new house? Yes, *he has*.
6 They have never *had* a dog.

4 1 Have you had pets?
2 Has he looked after children?
3 Has he been to Madrid?
4 Has she given you a present?

36 Hard work

1 1 clients   2 long hours   3 clients
4 a presentation   5 a meeting   6 a customer
7 a presentation   8 a decision

2 1 1 don't have to   2 have to (Picture B)
2 1 has to   2 Does; have to
3 has to (Picture C)
3 1 do; have to   2 have to
3 have to (Picture A)

37 Excuses, excuses

1 Across: 1 foot   3 hand   4 ear   7 stomach
Down: 2 throat   4 eye   5 arm   6 back

2 1 cough   2 headache   3 hurts
4 temperature   5 backache   6 sore throat
7 stomachache

3 1 A: I'm afraid I can't come to the cinema because I've got a temperature.
B: What a pity!
2 A: (I'm) sorry I can't help but I've hurt my back.
B: Don't worry!
3 A: (I'm) sorry I can't talk but I've got a sore throat.
B: That's OK!

38 Big issues

1 1 Transport   2 space   3 population
4 Communication   5 politics   6 climate

2 1 The climate will not change.
2 Cities will get smaller.
3 Where will you be next year?
4 He doesn't think he will be here.
5 People won't use public transport.

3 1 China will have the strongest economy.
2 Many people will speak Spanish.
3 In politics, there will be one world government.
4 Most people will drive flying cars.

39 Long life

1 For: two years; ages; over a month;
a long time; a couple of months; a week
Since: March; three o'clock; Tuesday; 17 July; 1980

2 1 Have you had your jacket for a long time?
2 How long has she lived there?
3 How long have they been on holiday?
4 Have they known you for ages?
5 Has he studied English for a long time?
6 How long have we been married?

3 a) 's studied   b) 's lived
c) 've been married   d) They 've been
e) 've had   f) haven't known

4 2 b   3 d   4 f   5 a   6 c

40 The perfect job

1 People: an employee; a boss; a colleague
Money: a salary; a pension
Places: an office; a gym; a créche

2 Dialogue 1: (1c)   2b   3a   4d
Dialogue 2: 1a   2d   3c   4b

3 1 What do you think?
2 (Yes,) that's true.
3 Do you agree?
4 In my opinion, money isn't everything.
5 (No,) I disagree.

Pearson Education Limited
Edinburgh Gate, Harlow
Essex CM20 2JE, England
and Associated Companies throughout the world

www.language-to-go.com

Language to go is a trademark of Pearson Education Limited

Second impression 2003

Set in 10/13pt Neue Helvetica Medium and 10/13pt Univers Light

Printed in Spain by Mateu Cromo, S. A. Pinto (Madrid).

ISBN 0 582 40396 0

Author acknowledgements

The authors would like to thank the Longman team and our fellow writers on the *Language to go* project for their help, encouragement and support. In particular, we would like to mention Bernie Hayden, who provided useful and entertaining feedback, Fran Banks for her meticulous and patient editing and Judith King for keeping the whole team in check.

We are also grateful to friends and colleagues at International House, London who have provided inspiration, support and kindness. In particular we would like to thank Roger Hunt for encouraging us to work on the project, Matthew Barnard, Glynn Jones and Jeremy Page.

On a more personal note, Simon le Maistre would like to thank Emily Wilkinson for her patience and constant support. Carina Lewis would like to thank Andrew Anderson for his patience and continual encouragement, which were invaluable while writing was in progress!

Publishing acknowledgements

The publishers would like to extend thanks to the freelance editorial team. We are indebted to Bernie Hayden, Senior Development Editor for the whole series and Project Manager of the Elementary and Pre-Intermediate levels, for his outstanding contribution to *Language to go*. Special thanks are due to Fran Banks for all her excellent work as editor. We would also like to acknowledge with thanks Kenna Bourke for her writing of the Grammar reference.

The publishers and authors are very grateful to the following people and institutions for reporting on the manuscript:

Wendy Abu-Saad, The New School of English, Cambridge; Steve Baxter, UK; Phyllis Vannuffel, ITS Hastings; Rolf Donald, Eastbourne School of English; Sarah Bailey, Lexis Instituto del Idioma; Málaga; Helen Hadkins, British Language Centre, Madrid; Stephanie Oliver, International House, Milan; James Tierney, The British Council, Milan; Anne Vernon James, IFG Langues, Paris; Philippa Dralet, Le Comptoir des Langues, Paris; Celso Frade, Evoluta Idiomas, São Paulo; Jennie Kober, Anglo English School, Hamburg; Nicholas Miller, Elvis Language School, Prague; Jodi Bennett, The Language House, Prague; Shaun Wilden, Akcent, IH Prague; Andrzej Antoszek, College of English/The Catholic University of Lublin, Poland; Patrycja Baran, College of English/The Catholic University of Lublin, Poland; Adam Kunysz, The Catholic University of Lublin/A1 School of Foreign Languages, Poland; Maria Eugenia Batista, Brazil; Christopher Reakirt, The New School of English, Cambridge.

We are grateful to the following for permission to reproduce copyright material:

Guinness Publishing Limited for an extract on the biggest Garfield collection in the world, published in *Guinness World Records 2000*.

Designed by Linda Reed & Associates.

Series design by Steve Pitcher.

Cover design by Juice Creative.

Illustrated by: Gary Andrews, Andy Baker (Début Art), Rowan Barnes Murphy, Kathy Baxendale, David Downton, Noel Ford, Mike Foster (The Maltings Partnership), Paul Hampson, Peter Lubach, Gillian Martin (The Art Market), Nicole Onslow (C II A), Chris Prout, Tony Richardson (The Wooden Ark), Debbie Ryder, Sue Tewkesbury, Geoff Waterhouse (Just for Laffs).

Picture research by Sally Smith.

We are grateful to the following for permission to reproduce copyright photographs:
Allsport for 20 (middle right), 21 (left, right); Anthony Blake Photo Library for 8 (middle left), 70 (bottom right); Art Directors and Trip for 52 (top right), 58 (bottom right), 78 (middle left bottom); Aspect Picture Library for 12/13 (top), 34; Corbis Images for 8 (middle right, top), 10 (top group: top left), 20 (middle left), 42 (bottom left), 60 (bottom left), 63 (bottom right), 78 (middle left), 80 (bottom right), 82 (bottom right); Greg Evans Picture Library for 10 (bottom group: bottom middle), 46 (top left), 49 (bottom left), 58 (bottom left); Getty Stone Images for 10 (bottom group: bottom left), 12 (top left), 20 (far left, far right), 39, 46 (bottom left), 59, 66 (middle left, bottom right), 70 (top left), 72 (bottom), 73, 74 (top right, middle left); 75 (bottom left); Ronald Grant Archive for 19; 30/31 (all); Robert Harding Picture Library for 38 (left), 58 (top right), 72 (top), 74 (bottom right); Hutchison Library for 78 (group: top left); Image Bank for 53 (bottom right); Image State for 10 (top group: top right, bottom group: bottom right), 10/11 (top), 17 (top left, middle right), 35, 45 (top left, bottom left), 52 top left; Impact Photos for 12 (bottom right), 53 (bottom left); Katz Pictures for 50, 78 (bottom right); Kobal Collection for 69 (middle right); Moviestore Collection for 42 (top right), 68 (bottom), 69 (top, bottom right), 78 (group: bottom); Network Photographers for 67; Pictor International for 10 (bottom group: top right), 58 (top left); The Photographers Library for 46 (left group: top right), 54 (top left), 60 (top left), 82 (top right); Popperfoto for 8 (bottom right); Graham Porter for 66 (top right); Powerstock Zefa for 24 (top right), 26 (bottom right), 54 (bottom), 55 (top), 63 (top left); Redferns for 80 (bottom left; Retna for p24 (bottom left), Rex Features for 18, 29, 43 (top right); Science Photo Library for 78 (group: middle right, middle left top, top right); Solo per Due for 60 (bottom right); The Stock Market for 26 (top right); Tony Stone for 4 (middle bottom); Topham Picturepoint for 17 (bottom left); Travel Ink for 26 (left).

Front cover photographs left to right: Powerstock Zefa; Powerstock Zefa; Pictor; Corbis Stock Market; Image State; Photo Disc.

We have been unsuccessful with our trace for the copyright holders of the image of Dodo Cheney on page 80; any help with this would be appreciated.

The following photographs were taken on commission for Pearson Education by:
Gareth Bowden for 10 (top group: middle top); Trevor Clifford for 4/5 (all), 6/7 (all), 8 (bottom left), 10 (top group: bottom left), 16 (all), 46 (right group: all), 48, 49 (top left), 62 (all), 82 (top left), 84 (all), 87 (all), 89 (all); James Walker for back cover photographs of the authors.